Life Story Therapy with Traumatized Children

by the same author

The Child's Own Story
Life Story Work with Traumatized Children
Richard Rose and Terry Philpot
Foreword by Mary Walsh, co-founder and Chief Executive of SACCS
ISBN 978 1 84310 287 8
eISBN 978 1 84642 056 6
Delivering Recovery series

of related interest

Creating Loving Attachments
Parenting with PACE to Nurture Confidence and Security in the Troubled Child
Kim S. Golding and Daniel A. Hughes
ISBN 978 1 84905 227 6
eISBN 978 0 85700 470 3

Attaching in Adoption
Practical Tools for Today's Parents
Deborah D. Gray
ISBN 978 1 84905 890 2
eISBN 978 0 85700 606 6

Nurturing Adoptions
Creating Resilience after Neglect and Trauma
Deborah D. Gray
ISBN 978 1 84905 891 9
eISBN 978 0 85700 607 3

Toddler Adoption
The Weaver's Craft
Mary Hopkins-Best
ISBN 978 1 84905 894 0
eISBN 978 0 85700 613 4

Life Story Books for Adopted Children
A Family Friendly Approach
Joy Rees
Foreword by Alan Burnell
Illustrated by Jamie Goldberg
ISBN 978 1 84310 953 2
eISBN 978 0 85700 190 0

Connecting with Kids through Stories
Using Narratives to Facilitate Attachment in Adopted Children
2nd edition
Denise B. Lacher, Todd Nichols, Melissa Nichols and Joanne C. May
ISBN 978 1 84905 869 8
eISBN 978 0 85700 454 3

Therapeutic Residential Care for Children and Young People
An Attachment and Trauma-Informed Model for Practice
Susan Barton, Rudy Gonzalez and Patrick Tomlinson
Foreword by Brian Burdekin
ISBN 978 1 84905 255 9
eISBN 9780857005380

Kenny Tasheck.

Life Story Therapy with Traumatized Children

A Model for Practice

Richard Rose
Foreword by Bruce D. Perry M.D., Ph.D.

Jessica Kingsley *Publishers*
London and Philadelphia

Quote on p.6 reprinted with permission from George Warren from ITV.
Quote on p.153 reprinted from *Harry Potter and the Philosopher's Stone* – Copyright © J.K. Rowling 1997 with the permission of the Blair Partnership.
Quote on p.154 reprinted from *Harry Potter and the Golbet of Fire* – Copyright © J.K. Rowling 2000 with the permission of the Blair Partnership.

First published in 2012
by Jessica Kingsley Publishers
116 Pentonville Road
London N1 9JB, UK
and
400 Market Street, Suite 400
Philadelphia, PA 19106, USA

www.jkp.com

Copyright © Richard Rose 2012
Foreword copyright © Bruce D. Perry 2012

All rights reserved. No part of this publication may be reproduced in any material form (including photocopying or storing it in any medium by electronic means and whether or not transiently or incidentally to some other use of this publication) without the written permission of the copyright owner except in accordance with the provisions of the Copyright, Designs and Patents Act 1988 or under the terms of a licence issued by the Copyright Licensing Agency Ltd, Saffron House, 6–10 Kirby Street, London EC1N 8TS. Applications for the copyright owner's written permission to reproduce any part of this publication should be addressed to the publisher.

Warning: The doing of an unauthorised act in relation to a copyright work may result in both a civil claim for damages and criminal prosecution.

Library of Congress Cataloging in Publication Data
Rose, Richard, 1965-
  Life story therapy with traumatized children : a model for practice / Richard Rose ; foreword by Bruce Perry.
     p. cm.
  Includes bibliographical references and index.
  ISBN 978-1-84905-272-6 (alk. paper)
 1. Psychic trauma in children--Treatment. 2. Narrative therapy. I. Title.
 RJ505.S75R67 2012
 618.92'8521--dc23
                             2012012674

British Library Cataloguing in Publication Data
A CIP catalogue record for this book is available from the British Library

ISBN 978 1 84905 272 6
eISBN 978 0 85700 574 8

Printed and bound in Great Britain

*For my wife Paula and my boys Ben and
Callum, who are the heroes in my life.*

Don't grow up angry Zoe. It takes so much effort to find your place in the world when you're angry, believe me.

From 'The Gift of Promise', a 'Lewis' feature, written by Dusty Hughes and Stephen Churchett.

Contents

Foreword by Bruce D. Perry 9
ACKNOWLEDGEMENTS   12
PREFACE   13

Part I: The Roots of Life Story Therapy 17

1. Introducing Life Story Therapy 18
2. The Developing Brain, the Body, Trauma and Attachment 36
3. Preparing for Life Story Therapy 60

Part II: The Stages of Life Story Therapy . . . 75

4. Stage 1: The Information Bank 76
5. Stage 2: Direct Work with Children 98
6. Stage 3: Understanding the Process 127
7. Internalization 142
8. The Life Story Book and Outcomes 157
9. Alice: A life story journey 169
   REFERENCES   176
   INTERNET ACCESSED MATERIAL   180
   FURTHER READING   181
   SUBJECT INDEX   183
   AUTHOR INDEX   187

List of Figures

Figure 2.1 Three nerve cells (neurons). 38
Figure 2.2 Illustration of the brain and functions 40
Figure 4.1 Jade's story in movement boxes 80
Figure 4.2 Jade's story: ecomaps. 82
Figure 4.3 Using movement boxes to help clarify understanding: Step 1 94
Figure 4.4 Using movement boxes to help clarify understanding: Step 2 96
Figure 5.1 Life story session plan 101
Figure 5.2 Life story session outcomes appraisal. 102
Figure 5.3 Graph showing feelings for a week 110
Figure 5.4 Feelings symbolized in terms of 'food'. 111
Figure 5.5 'All About Me' book 113
Figure 5.6 'Fact, Fiction, Fantasy and Heroism' template 120
Figure 5.7 'Fact, Fiction, Fantasy and Heroism': an example. 126
Figure 6.1 Preoccupation 127
Figure 6.2 Preoccupation explained 129
Figure 6.3 'Behaviour Tree': words on foliage 131
Figure 6.4 Leaf and bubble work 132
Figure 6.5 'Behaviour Tree': the roots 132
Figure 6.6 The completed 'Behaviour Tree' 133
Figure 6.7 Good things about life story 136
Figure 6.8 Bad things about life story 136
Figure 6.9 Fight and flight actions. 139
Figure 6.10 Fight and flight contained 141
Figure 7.1 'Fact, Fiction, Fantasy and Heroism' 145
Figure 7.2 Example of a skeletal family tree 147
Figure 7.3 The thinking game. 150
Figure 8.1 Radial grid shape created for John 168

Foreword

A fundamental and permeating strength of humankind is the capacity to form and maintain relationships – the capacity to belong. It is in the context of our clan, community and culture that we are born and raised. The brain-mediated set of complex capacities that allow one human to connect to another form the very basis for survival and has led to the 'success' of our species on this planet. Without others or without belonging, no individual could survive or thrive. This need is so biologically powerful that when an infant is given signals from his caregivers that he is 'not wanted' and does not belong, the brain's neural networks will activate a 'shut down' response and induce a 'failure to thrive.' And even with calories (but without the physical manifestations of 'love') this infant will lose weight and may die. This early life manifestation of the power of belonging has many related neurophysiological features later in life; the stress response and 'reward' networks in our brain are all interwoven with our 'relational' neurobiology. When familiar and welcoming human interactions are present, we feel pleasure and safety; we are regulated, we belong. When we are disconnected, when we are marginalized, we feel distressed, we literally feel pain.

This powerful, regulating, rewarding quality of belonging to a group, a family, a community and culture is not just focused on the present. We each feel a need to be connected to the people of our past; and without being able to draw on this connection – this narrative – it is almost impossible to envision hopes and dreams for a connected and safe future. It is the very part of our brain that is most uniquely human, the neocortex, that allows us to store, sort and recall our past as we construct the narrative that becomes the pathway from the past, and it is also the neocortex that envisions our pathways into the future. The neocortex allows humans to tell time; to create complex symbolic representations and associations that we have transformed into various forms of language; in music, art, writing (all inventions of our past) we are able to re-tell our story. The story of our people, where we come from and how we belong; our cortex helps us process, sort and sequence events and to store both our personal experience and the narrated experiences of others; the story of our parents; our parent's story of our childhood before we could make narrative memory; the story of their parents; the history of how we belong.

Storytelling is a unique and permeating quality present in all cultures across every era. The first and universal function of narrative in song, ceremony and story is how we have come to be, where we are connected, where we belong, where the connections were broken, lost, repaired. And in the cortically mediated narrative of storytelling of how we belong and how we have come to this point comes a powerful regulating, anchoring, reassuring and rewarding neurophysiological effect. It is no surprise that humans, the storytelling primates, are fascinated by narrative, poetry, novels and movies. The majority of our arts will portray personal narrative in some fashion.

This crucial aspect of the human condition – belonging, knowing your narrative – is damaged for many. And damaging the narrative of a people (cultural genocide) is at the core of a destructive, transgenerational process that has many negative manifestations; as odd as this may sound, the neurobiological consequences of stripping a community or culture of their language, customs, religious beliefs or child-rearing practices are devastating. The individual stress response systems and 'reward' neurobiology in a marginalized, disconnected and culturally fragmented group will be compromised and predisposes individuals of that group to a host of mental (e.g., depression, suicide), physical (e.g., diabetes) and social (e.g., increased substance abuse) problems. This is seen in Aboriginal communities in Australia, First Nations communities in Canada and Māori communities in New Zealand, among others. The neurobiological consequences of the destruction of narrative for a people are devastating.

It is the same with individual maltreated children. A fragmented, damaged, discontinuous personal narrative puts an individual child at risk. A child that is lost within her own family, community and culture is neurodevelopmentally vulnerable. Without a life story, a child is adrift, disconnected and vulnerable – *their neurobiology of reward, stress regulation and relational interactions are all altered – in negative ways – without a cortically mediated coherent personal narrative.* Our conventional efforts to 'treat' them will often be frustrated and ineffective. Sadly, most mental health interventions with maltreated children do not pay any attention to the child's story. The focus is the manifestation of pathology – the symptoms. Make Billy stop swearing, hitting, running away – make Billy pay attention, be respectful, comply. We lose sight of how disconnected Billy is and often we actually contribute to the fragmentation and disconnection of his life story – a brief but telling story to illustrate how our efforts to 'protect' maltreated children can add to their confusion and disconnection. We often make these children worse.

At the beginning of an evaluation of a ten-year-old boy in foster care at our ChildTrauma Academy clinic, I asked him his name:

> 'Which name do you want to know?'
> 'What do you mean?'
> 'Well, I don't know my name, I guess. My new mum calls me Thomas. My last mum called me Leon. And when I visit my grandmother she calls me Robbie.'
> 'What name do you tell your friends to call you?'
> 'I don't have any friends at this new house.'
> 'Do you know what your biological mother named you?'
> 'I think she named me Baby.'

As I looked through the records I could see that he was born a few weeks early. He had been in the Pediatric ICU and had never been named by his mother. His discharge records stated: 'Baby Boy Jones'. Ten placements and four 'names' meant he was disconnected and adrift with no personal narrative. But 'fix him' if he acts out. He is inattentive, disrespectful, struggles in school and won't do as he's told. Fix him. Find the right label. Give him the right drug. Our current approach to these maltreated children has lost sight of the essential element of healing – and that is reconnection. Connect to the present and increase the number and quality of relational opportunities but, as important, reconstruct your past connections, lay out your disconnects and clarify your personal journey to the present.

The value and power of the life story approach to reconstructing and reconnecting a child using personal narrative cannot be underestimated and the way that Richard Rose lays out the core elements of this approach is both practical and elegant. This is a refreshing and renewing clinical approach that is both developmentally sensitive and 'trauma-informed.' It echoes the fundamental storytelling powers known to our ancestors who incorporated storytelling into all of their healing practices and rituals – in other words, storytelling therapy reflects not just knowledge of human healing, it is a manifestation of wisdom about humankind. For any clinician working with our most disconnected children this is a wonderful way to help them reconnect – and heal.

Bruce D. Perry, M.D., Ph.D.
Senior Fellow, The ChildTrauma Academy, Houston, TX
Adjunct Professor, Department of Psychiatry and Behavioral Sciences,
Feinberg School of Medicine, Northwestern University, Chicago, IL

Acknowledgements

I am especially grateful to Mary Walsh, co-founder and chair of Sexual Abuse Child Consultancy Service (SACCS), for her continuing support, investment, and above all, faith in my practice and activities over the last 15 years. We have literally travelled the world in our desire to influence and be influenced by best practice and I will always acknowledge her dedication to the healing of traumatized children.

The book is also informed, most significantly of course, by the work that I have undertaken over the last 28 years in the field of child and family care. The children, parents, families and my colleagues across the world have provided so much opportunity to create a therapeutic approach with the evidential outcomes that we all require to validate our intervention.

I am grateful to 'Britney' and Maxine Eccleston for their contribution to the feedback from intervention within a school environment, and also grateful to the young people who have contributed to content within the book. They know who they are and I am sure that their contribution will assist practitioners in providing the very best support to children who have experienced the kind of harm that they have.

Thanks are also due to Jill Hughes, an extremely dedicated social worker, for the work we have done on the SHANARRI (Safe, Healthy, Active, Nurtured, Achieving, Respected, Responsible and Included) evaluation and outcome model. I would like to express my gratitude to Emmeley Raphael for her contribution to the book and for the support from Paula Price, newly qualified life story therapist. As in the previous book, I would formally like to acknowledge SACCS' life story work team at Shrewsbury and Tamworth, with special mention of Rachel Oliver, who has continued to promote best practice in life story since 2000.

The names of all children and adults in the case studies have been changed and some details have been altered to protect anonymity, but it is important to point out that no details have been invented. The children and adults referred to in this book are between three and 45 years of age, and so I will refer to those under 18 as 'children' and those over 18 as 'adults'. For ease of reading, I refer to children in the feminine and adults (whether staff, parents or others) in the masculine – unless, of course, I am referring to specific cases and situations.

Preface

At the start of this book on life story therapy, I'd like to include a little detail about my own story and the story behind the book.

About me

I began my social work career in 1984 when I was appointed a residential care worker for a children's home in Swindon. I obtained a Certificate of Qualification in Social Work (CQSW) and Diploma in Social Studies in 1989 and worked in a child and family team in Swindon. In 1991 I moved to Shropshire to become the senior social worker in Shropshire's child protection team, and became a practice teacher in 1996.

In 1997 I left the statutory services and was employed with Sexual Abuse Child Consultancy Service (SACCS) as a life story practitioner. SACCS started life as a consultancy service and has now been in existence for 25 years, with a reputation as a leading residential therapeutic service for traumatized children.

The work described within this book is representative of the work I have been involved in at SACCS. SACCS has always regarded the children that have engaged in the recovery work as normal children who have had abnormal experiences. In essence: children are not monsters; they have had monstrous things happen to them and sometimes these monstrous things are replicated by them as they communicate their trauma.

From 1997 onwards, the organization invested substantially in the evolving intervention of life story work and in 2002 I began to speak nationally about the positive effects of therapeutic life story, which led to further conferences and training programmes. I looked at conventional life story work and found it inadequate for the work that SACCS wished to do with the children in its care.

At the time of writing (in 2011) I am engaged by SACCS to deliver therapeutic life story work with up to 30 children in their home environments throughout the UK, and have recently founded a new service for traumatized children and their families and for those caring for the most vulnerable within our community: Child Trauma Intervention

Services, which is dedicated to providing consultancy, supervision, guidance and teaching in the UK and internationally on areas of child and family trauma and life story therapy.

About this book

In 2004 I co-authored with Terry Philpot a book called *The Child's Own Story: Life Story Work with Traumatized Children*, which aimed to communicate the work we did at SACCS for professionals to understand and to incorporate the various techniques to assist children to explore, question and resolve issues and events within their life journey. It was based on the SACCS approach to life story within a residential programme involving the recovery team approach – this being life story work, therapeutic parenting and therapy. The techniques and intervention were centred round the premise of holistic care of the child in stable, intensive environments.

Life Story Therapy for Traumatized Children aims to build upon the ideas introduced in *The Child's Own Story*, and also to show how life story therapy can be considered a form of therapy in its own right. As you read it, I hope that you begin to understand the potential of the intervention and find the practice, the theory and the activities useful and creative for your own role and professional approach.

The content of the book is based on interventions which can be employed within the community, be that a school, a foster home, adoption setting or the parental home. I also consider a life story therapy approach with parents of children who are within or on the verge of care and how such intervention can be both cost effective and provide positive lifelong benefits to children and their families.

Everyone has a story: their perception of what, where, when, who, why and how. Our stories are what make us – we are, after all, what we were. In acknowledging this simple truth, we can look to the future with acceptance of the now and the expectation of a healthier tomorrow.

The role of the life story therapist is to undertake the task of a jigsaw-solver: to collect the pieces of the jigsaw, scattered to the four winds, and carefully piece these together to create as clear a picture as possible. Then, using gentle encouragement, the child is asked 'Can you see it, can you see it yet?' The jigsaw of a complex life will always have pieces missing, but if we treat each piece carefully we can, with the help of the child, fit those we have together to create a view which allows reflection, accepts distortion and permits reframing around the final picture.

I am often asked how long life story takes. This book will explore the context of the intervention, the process and the application; but the reality is that it will take as long as it takes.

Children who have been traumatized often carry this trauma and their understanding of the root causes of the same in their internal world. Their external communication of this trauma is as individual as the children themselves, and the approach of the therapist also needs to be as individual and unique as the children themselves.

It is for this reason that I do not advocate using templates, computer-generated life story work or 'All About Me' books off the shelf. All the work, in my view, needs to be created with and by the child, the carer and the therapist.

I hope that this book sets out the credentials of life story therapy as an approach that merits a place among the accepted and more traditional therapies that are often referred to as 'talking therapies'. Unlike many of these, which are by design non-directive and worker-interpretive, this approach is directive and participant-interpretive.

I base all my interventions on the premise that 'If you want to know what is wrong with someone, ask them'. The relevance of this approach extends beyond its application to trauma work and in later chapters I will explore the application of techniques developed for life story therapy in education and social care.

My intention for this book is for it to be used as a resource for therapeutic application and as a guide to exploration of a new therapy, being an invitation not just to social workers but to all those involved in supporting the recovery of children.

> The journey to recovery is a long one and it belongs to the child. The child is at the centre of everything we do – a principle exemplified by life story work. (Walsh 2004)

Part I

The Roots of Life Story Therapy

Chapter 1

Introducing Life Story Therapy

We are what we were

> It is difficult to grow up as a psychologically healthy adult if one is denied access to one's own history. (Fahlberg 2008)

The phrase 'life story work' is commonly used in the social care field, to indicate that an intervention around the history of the child is undertaken. Children placed in the care of a local authority, in permanence or long-term, are entitled to be given information about their past, their birth family, culture and heritage. The UK government has endorsed this view through the Care Matters agenda presented to Parliament in 2007, which itself stems from the Every Child Matters legislation within the Children Act 2004.

> It is essential that professionals involved in supporting children and carers have a strong understanding of attachment and of the importance of core practice such as life story work (where a child is helped to make sense of their past experiences) so that they may help an abused, harmed or neglected child to develop a secure emotional base. It is also important that children, carers and professionals have access to appropriate therapeutic interventions that can address the damage that previous experiences have caused to a child's ability to form attachments. (Care Matters Time for Change 2007)

Life story work, however, is not standardized; therefore a child's experience of the intervention is wholly dependent on the practitioner's awareness of the process, the time available to the practitioner and the importance attached to the task, relative to other demands on the individuals involved. I am not in favour of life story work being carried out by students on social work and social care practice placements, although there are wonderful opportunities to engage them in detective roles in the context of creating information banks. Life story requires relationship building and working at the child's pace, but placements do not afford the time for this to happen, and it is important that anyone engaged in the process is there for the entirety of the work.

The next issue is to decide what form of life story is the most appropriate. A child who has settled well in placement and has developed attachment to her carers may not benefit from an experience of therapeutic life story or life history work. A child who is at risk of placement breakdown, who may feel insecure and confused about her family and her future, may also not benefit from an experience of story work or basic life history work.

Assessment of children is an essential first step; it may be that the adult agenda is to 'do life story' but it may be the last thing that the child would want. A detailed assessment will help the practitioner to look behind the presentation, consider the role of the carers, identify the real issues and, if appropriate, support the child to see that the activity would provide a positive outcome for her. Not all children will benefit from the process. For some this may be a permanent issue, for many it is in the timing. The importance, for children, of the opportunity to think about and explore their roots, their growth and their sense of self depends on their willingness to engage.

I have had the opportunity to talk about life story in four continents, and each has a view of the importance of family history, of storytelling through the generations, which enriches and embeds the present with the past. In Seattle, at Day Break Star, a centre for culture and celebration, the organization United Indians of All Tribes provides programmes for all sections of the community. One of these programmes relates to the importance of the relationship between the elder (grandparent or third age) and the child, in which the focus is on the telling of stories past, and how the children themselves become the vessel for the future. There was a particular saying that I was introduced to when delivering life story training in Seattle, USA and on Vancouver Island, Canada to the Indigenous peoples:

> We recognize our relationship to the past and to our future because they are the same thing. (Winona LaDuke, Anishinabe, date unknown)

In the UK most residential and foster care providers now include a life story service to children. The approaches are varied: some include a therapeutic element, others introduce a life story 'box' to capture the child's journey whilst in that placement. This seems to have been particularly successful in projects such as the 'Memory Store' based in Northumberland and presented by Gillian Shotton (2010) in her article 'Telling different stories: the experience of foster/adoptive carers in carrying out collaborative memory work with children'. Other organizations use electronic and pro-forma books.

In Sydney, Australia, workers in Metro Intensive Support Services are provided with a life story folder for Indigenous and for non-Indigenous children. This includes prompting sheets, and dividers for personal, family and friends information, and can be tailored to meet the individual child's needs.

In some forms of life story work, the child's story is collated. It may then be discussed with the child before a book is produced, which presents a chronological illustration of her life journey.

Sadly, more commonly, 'life story' is a collation of 'known facts' about a child, contained in a short book which represents so little of the child's real story and so much of the social work recorded file history.

The experience of some children who are recommended life story work is that work commences, but through no fault of their own the professional moves to a new role and the intervention is delayed, or even dropped – consigned to the unfinished work pile, never to be picked up again.

I am currently involved in providing direct work with children in the UK. These children are from various regions and all have complex needs which affect their placement and their relationship with their carers, and present behaviours which risk the placement stability. I also work with two adoption programmes, one in Argyll and Bute and one in South Gloucestershire, on issues of identity and life story work. The children I work with range from 3 to 16 years of age. The majority are female and have difficult histories which need to be explored and then made sense of, to enable them to separate themselves from their sense of guilt and shame. Most of the children are in placements and have had a myriad of previous interventions which, for whatever reason, have not been successful. Some of these cases have past review recommendations which state that life story work is required or underway, but rarely has such work been carried out, and when it has been done, its effectiveness has often proved limited – often due to the kinds of circumstances described above.

Clearly, 'life story work' is a term that means different things to different people, so I'll now attempt to define the approach advocated within this book. I have observed three types of life story used within the social care field today. Each has a valid application, but each can also cause difficulty for the child who is the subject of the work.

1. Story work

This approach is based on the recollection of the child and her understanding of the events in her life. It is akin to reminiscence work, where the facilitator is interested in hearing the 'narrative' of the subject child and not concerned with the stories of others. Often the work is carried out as a one-to-one process, and the facilitator will incorporate 'date' evidence for 'discussion points'; these would include things such as music, photographs and documents, including birth certificates and newspaper cuttings.

Positive applications with this approach include the opportunity for the child to tell her story and to be heard. Children are not confronted by inaccuracies, poor memory recollection or confusion as they are encouraged to consider their perception, which is given value and thereby validated.

This approach is regularly found to occur when facilitators begin life story work from the moment the child is placed in the care system. Of course this is the only approach that can be adopted if the facilitator only has information that begins from the moment that the child arrives in the care placement. (It is not surprising that the facilitator is often the foster carer of the child concerned.)

> ### Case study: Callum
> Callum is an 11-year-old child who has experienced acute neglect by his parents from as early as he can remember. He was made subject to care proceedings following a drug search at his family home. The officers who arrived at the scene found the home to be poorly cared for, with drug paraphernalia, including needles and substances, located in the bedroom of Callum and his baby stepsister. Callum had been subject to various child protection enquiries and had been cared for in the past by extended family and through voluntary arrangements under Section 20 of the Children Act 1989.

> A life story book was completed for Callum when he was 9; it consisted of 11 pages and 8 photographs. The story basically detailed an incomplete and sadly inaccurate family tree, his brief 'pen picture' memory of his mother and stepfather, and his conclusion that he had been placed in care due to his naughty behaviour and because his 'mum chose her boyfriend over him and his sister'. There was an account of his time with his carers, in which it was stated that he felt happy living with them and that he was there forever.

In this case, Callum was heard and his book did represent his memory; however there was very little detail, meaning or understanding of the reasoning and action of those who had responsibility for him. He was proud of his book, but he had a conviction that he was responsible for being placed in care. When considering Callum's history as described in the above case study, unanswered questions (Why he was unsafe? Who had hurt him? Why was he placed in care?) are clearly identifiable, but the story work approach that was utilized did not allow such exploration to take place. Callum's placement did not last 'forever' and he has just been placed in his fourth home since the completion of his story work.

The story work approach relies on the child's memory and perceptions. If these are internalized as the 'unshakeable truth' and accepted by the listener as valid, then the child's willingness to consider a different story, which may be a more truthful account, is far more difficult to achieve. Story work cannot provide the 'full history' of the child; it cannot introduce the pre-birth history, the first few years of her life, her internal working model or the essential need for her to consider her past in comparison with her present.

The danger of this approach is that the child can be given assurance and the conviction that all she remembers is accurate, factual and conclusive. The memory may then be adopted as 'the whole truth and nothing but the truth', and for some children, therefore, the unshakeable story of their life.

My subsequent work with Callum addressed the need to 'unpick' the story contained in his 'book', and to provide safety and security for him to reframe his understanding of his own role and the role of others.

Story work can, however, be useful for intervention that does not require a full life story/history approach. I have used the process of story work to assist children to tell their story, as a means to aid thinking and drawing conclusions about selected events or 'slices' within their personal history. I have referred to this as 'spot' work; the intervention is concentrated on a particular issue, event or crisis, and is particularly effective when working with placement disruption, school disruption and contact difficulties, and working with wishes and feelings.

2. Life history work

Life history work is often referred to as 'life story work'. However, in most cases the approach does not involve the child in the process. A clear example of this is found in the adoption 'life story book' – a book created to enable the child to understand in future years why he or she is subject to an adoption order.

Life history work is a process that gives the child the opportunity to understand her history; it is often provided by a social worker, foster carer or student, and aims to provide a written account of the child's life journey from her birth to the present date. Life history work has been widely considered as a default service for children who are subject to adoption, and latterly for children who are placed in permanency.

As early as 1981 Aust introduced the notion of life story books as helpful for children in placement, followed by Backhaus (1984), who proposed that life story books could be a tool for working with children in care. Fahlberg (1994) and Ryan and Walker (1993) promoted life story work as a beneficial process for children in foster care and adoption. Terry Philpot and I (Rose and Philpot 2005) introduced life story as a therapeutic tool for recovery work with traumatized children, and Joy Rees (2009) introduced life story techniques for adoption life story books. Life story work has been encouraged as a way of providing children with a narrative which explains life events and the sequence of their journey from before their birth to the current placement in which they find themselves.

In life history work, in order to secure this narrative, the child does not have the opportunity to explore her own understanding of events, or to talk about those who have had significant impact on her life and the role of guilt, shame and responsibility within it. Much life history work consists of collating 'easy-to-find' information which is often untested, and taken as truthful. This collated information is placed within a story, loosely based on a chronology, and then presented, often as a completed piece of work, to the child.

Most of us who have been employed in social services will acknowledge in our more relaxed moments that our recording in files, often carried out days after the recorded events, was not as accurate as we would like it to have been. Accounts of these events are often based on opinion and therefore subjective; and again, most children within the social care system would have experienced multiple placements and experiences of social worker change. As an example, during the time I have been working with one young person this year, he has had five different social workers, each with a slightly different approach and slightly different beliefs and ethical stances. It is highly probable that this has led to different conclusions about problems, and consequently to different thinking and proposed solutions for the child's best interest, and inconsistencies in recording.

It is clear that much life history work is collated from social work files and re-interpreted for the child in a life story book (which, all being well, is also age-appropriate).

I have had the opportunity to view hundreds of life story books. In most case, they are valued dearly by the child and their carers. These books vary, from a few written pages, to photograph albums, to beautifully created stories; whichever sort the child receives often depends entirely on the professional involved, the time they had and the commitment and skills they brought to the task.

Such life story books often fail to include the difficult situations that are often the very reason for the child being placed in the care of people outside their families. They may be lovingly produced for the child, but relate only the positive events and not the abuse, the death or the more 'ugly' sides of the child's experience. I once worked with a 13-year-old child who was keen to show me her life story book. It was a series of photographs, with a paragraph, or a few lines of information about each picture. The child was able to tell me who was who, and what their relationship was to her, but she was not able to connect the pictures of the people or the places to the story of her life. She was not able to identify who did what to whom and when, where and why it had happened, or its connection to her experiences of abuse, her care episodes, her adoption or its subsequent breakdown.

I have worked with parents of children who have been placed within the care system, who explain how such life story books, far from helping their children, have caused more sadness, more difficulty and distress. One parent explained that a social worker delivered her child's life story book to the child on a contact visit. Once she had handed over the book, she announced that she (the social worker) was leaving the authority. The child, on receiving the book, immediately flicked through it to find out who her father was, and found that this information had not been included. She turned to the social worker and asked her why not, and was told 'You're old enough to know, ask your mother.' At this the child turned to ask, and the parent stood up and left the room, and the contact session was stopped.

Life story books are often completed on behalf of the child, especially for children who are under three years of age. These approaches may not be as helpful as they are currently considered to be. They may contain sparse information which proves unhelpful. I have seen many such books and frequently they have photographs of people (sadly, some of these photographs are labelled incorrectly); there is an absence of a clear story line and a few statements from persons involved, which say more about future wishes than past realities. In later life, when the child begins to ask questions about her identity, the life story book does not contain the detail that is needed to provide the answers.

I have previously made the case for replacing life story books with 'moving from and moving in' books for adoption and permanency placements for children under three. A 'moving from and moving in' book is a collated record of the child's journey from the pre-adoption placement to the adoption placement. The 'moving from' part should ideally contain a series of photographs of significant people and events in the child's life (accurately labelled), with a memory bubble from each containing a positive memory of the child. There should be a simple paragraph detailing why the 'movement from' is taking place, and a calendar of the events which led up to the pre-adoption placement ending and the adoption placement beginning. The 'moving in' section should include a welcome from the new family, with significant pictures of the people who will form the new family unit. Again, each picture should have a speech bubble which welcomes the child and expresses offers of support and care. A calendar of the first month of the placement should be included. (The child and carers complete this as the placement proceeds.)

In 2006 the Commission for Social Care Inspection conducted a survey of young people who had been adopted, with respect to the areas of confusion, if any, around their past (Morgan 2006). It found that children wanted to know why they could not stay with their birth families; who the people were who gave birth to them; what had happened to them in the past; about their birth and other relatives, particularly siblings. These details are basic, yet hold countless other stories which, when handled safely, can provide assurance, stability and hope to all involved. In an article for the BBC Roger Morgan, the Children's Rights Director, quoted a child interviewed by his team, who said that:

It was important to know your history...you can't just wipe away the past. (BBC 2006)

3. Life story therapy (therapeutic life story work)

The third form of life story work which I have observed is that which forms the subject for this book. Over the years I have been involved in developing approaches which assist children to engage in direct work that affords an explorative narrative of their life and that of their parents and grandparents.

As detailed in the preface to this book, *The Child's Own Story* (Rose and Philpot 2005) described a life story approach within the structure of a residential therapeutic children's facility, but in the years since then I have developed a more flexible approach with wider application, which can be effective in working with children and adults within a community setting. This approach has formed the basis of MA and diploma courses in life story therapy (offered by the Sexual Abuse Child Consultancy Service (SACCS) in partnership with Liverpool Hope University, UK).

Life story therapy is a defined approach which provided the opportunity for children to explore their history and the wider history of their family, and to do this with their carer so that both can develop their knowledge of each other and begin to understand the behaviours, feelings and cognitive processes that manifest themselves within placement. The therapy is designed to introduce the past as a set of markers for the present. Once these are understood, then the child is supported in considering if she wants to be led by the past events, or to make significant changes as a result of her new awareness.

This book considers the impact of a child's early life experience on the architecture of the brain. If it is accepted that the brain is the 'organ of behaviour' (NIH Massachusetts 2005), then the more that can be identified with the child with regard to her early life experiences, the more she can understand about her current behaviours and where they may originate from. Once this is identified, the child is helped to think it through, to consider the unconscious thinking expressed through her actions, and whether these automatic responses can be tamed and more thought-led actions taken.

In essence, life story therapy is not just about the who, what, where, when, why and how of events – it is also about the consequences of those events, and how they drive the child, and present issues and difficulties. On many occasions I have witnessed children suddenly realizing that what they do, and why, when, where, who they do it to/with and how they do it, connects to repetitive patterns of their past. This realization is then worked with, and reshaping, reframing and real change take place. As the therapy is delivered alongside the carer, the transformation is not just for the child, it also affects the carer.

I have on many occasions been asked if the intervention of life story causes the child to become re-traumatized. I do not feel that this occurs if the therapy is carried out sensitively and confidently. The majority of children I work with carry their trauma; it has not gone away, and instead tends to seep out now and then and create great difficulty for them if not addressed and dealt with. When I first came to work at SACCS, I remember a sign outside one of the doors which talked of monsters and rainbows. The famous horror and thriller writer Stephen King proposed in his introduction to the bestselling book *The Shining* (2002) that monsters and ghosts live within us. He argued that sometimes they succeed despite our desire to fight them. Often, when I am working with children who are aggressive and hurtful, they express their regret and sadness for the actions they rely on when feeling scared, anxious and/or out of control. These regrets are often voiced as, 'I couldn't stop myself, my inside feelings had to break out and I can't control those feelings'. If we can help children to think about their trauma, to understand its origins, its purpose and its effects, we can label the ghosts of the past and the monsters inside. In achieving this we support the child and their carers to promote the child's best interest.

> A major aspect of direct work is listening for the child's perceptions. Until we do this, we won't know if we are to expand their information or correct their misperceptions. (Fahlberg 1994)

In listening to perceptions, and in valuing children's experience, we are exploring the events of children's lives, and this includes the 'good, the bad and the ugly'. Fahlberg, again, states:

> The very fact that adults hesitate to share information about the past with a child implies to him that his past is so bad that he won't be able to cope with it. Whatever the past was – the child lived through it and survived, and so can live with the truth. The truth can be presented in a harmful way that lowers the child's self-esteem or in a way that helps the child to understand and accept his past and thus raises his self-esteem. (Fahlberg 1981)

Life story therapy is different from story work or life history work, because it works with children and their primary carers from the beginning of the process to the end. It is designed to work on the relationship between the carer and the child by inviting both to consider the events of the child's individual journey and that of their family of origin. I detail the process by stages below.

The stages of life story therapy

1. First stage: The information bank

The first stage is the creation of an 'information bank' to build a clear understanding of the child's pre-birth and post-birth history. This develops chronologically and includes evidence, both physical and written, which becomes the basis of the interaction. Such an approach requires the worker to collate the information, consider the validity and usefulness of the material, and then interview those involved to gain a historical perspective.

The information bank does not rely upon the social work file, as that forms only part of the story. It should include parental contributions and health information, particularly centred on the child's early years history, which will allow the worker to consider her 'internal working model' and 'attachment' issues. (These concepts are defined in greater detail later in the book. See Chapter 2, page 52)

The collation of physical evidence can include pictures, first toys and books and perhaps the 'red book'. (In the UK the red book (the full title of which is the Personal Child Health Record) is kept by the birth parent or primary carer, and encourages the carer to record the weight and height of their child, as well as the developmental milestones achieved. These milestones include crawling, walking, teething and talking.) In Oregon, USA, the authorities have introduced a screening programme which is called the Healthy Start – Healthy Families (HS/HF) service.

> HS/HF attempts to reach all consenting first-birth parents to offer screening, referral, and information. Families may also receive a Welcome Baby gift packet filled with information about parenting and child development. (Oregon Commission on Children and Families 2011)

In Australia, the Personal Health Record is referred to as the 'blue book', and its function, as with the others above, is to record the child's development. For the life story therapist, this book, be it blue, red or colours in-between, is extremely valuable to the child, especially if the child has little opportunity to recapture these events directly from her parent.

The personal health record of development, alongside the birth certificate, are helpful discussion points for the child to consider her life journey and to discuss how she in turn might care for others in the future. This can be further enhanced with the acquisition of first toys and books, and perhaps early photographs. It is also a positive way to demonstrate that the life story process is a journey which invites exploration and discussion.

Good information banks also provide essential information for those who are decision makers for the child – not just social workers, but also educators, carers and health professionals. By taking time to understand where the child has come from and what part people have played in her life, the worker can begin to plan the intervention and share appropriate information with those who have care of her.

2. Second stage: Internalization

Once a clear information bank is created, the life story process can move on to the second stage, called 'internalization'.

> Internalisation is about dealing with feelings and the child's inner life, children should be allowed to present what they wish to present, to express what they wish to express. It is not necessary to agree with all they say, or how they think or feel, and a worker may know that something which a child has said is not correct, but it is essential that what is said or felt is respected. (Rose and Philpot 2005)

To achieve internalization, the child has to be encouraged first to externalize her thoughts, feelings and emotions. This externalization is then debated, explored and recorded on wallpaper (as discussed in Chapter 7). The process of internalizing the story is carried out as the child reaches an understanding that is reframed and acceptable. It will include the bad and the ugly sides of life, but these will be reframed and accepted as a part of the child's past, and not the story of the present and the future. The ideal internalization is one where the child reaches acceptance of who she was, who she is, and a clear understanding that she has the power to shape who she can be.

It is essential that life story work is delivered alongside the primary carer, since this provides a multitude of benefits, chief among them emotional support for the child, the creation of a safe environment alongside a familiar and caring adult and emotional containment, so as to encourage the life story therapist to facilitate the intervention, and not to engage in the emotional context that the child and/or the carer need to engage in. The development of this relationship between the carer and the child will be facilitated, promoting understanding and growth by inviting both to consider and explore the events of the child's life and what that has meant for the child's current world.

Typically this second stage will take about 12 to 18 sessions, and if done well, the facilitated work will support the placement and the commitment between the carer and the child. The detail held within the information bank can be broken into session plans, and any work carried out in this fashion should be done fortnightly, each session lasting not more than an hour. The internalization process includes 'wishes and feelings' work, exploration of feelings and the vocabulary and behavioural representation of these. Over the course of the internalization, the life story therapist begins to unravel the story of the child, starting with the grandparents and moving through the life of the grandparents to the birth of her parents. This will allow the child the opportunity to think about families, who they are and where they come from, and to record what she thinks about them and their actions. As the journey continues, the child is introduced to her parents (on paper). The parents' childhood, issues, sad times and happy times are discussed. Often, children will begin to recognize patterns in their lives that are similar to those of their parents. This is explored and thoughts are shared as to what could have happened differently and how things might have changed. Children can often identify the mistakes that their parent has made, the choices that led to poor outcomes. All are explored, thought through and recorded in the first person; it is my experience that children will often have completed two rolls of wallpaper before the process reaches their own birth.

The interaction continues chronologically as the child builds a fuller picture of her life and the twists and turns that it has taken. As King (2001) suggests, memories are like the ghosts of our lives, they have a habit of shadowing our present and sometimes, when we are less in control of the present, our actions are led by these ghosts. In doing so, the past has the ability to guide us, and this guidance can adversely affect the decisions and actions that we take. By encouraging the child to consider her feelings with particular regard to past events we can identify and understand some of those memories (ghosts) and start to unpack the aura around these. We are able to then compare these to present day experiences and consider what is safe and what is unsafe. It is always helpful to observe with the child and the carer how the introduction of empathy and appropriate sadness, as well as joy can be rekindled from the past and moved safely into the present and become a resource for the future.

The wallpaper work continues as the child explores her story, and in the course of this she may revisit the previous work and put two and two together and make four. This is sequencing, which to me is the main aim of this approach. When a child can identify sequence on wallpaper, and see that one thing led to another and to another and to another, she can reflect on the events of her current life and begin to identify the sequencing that exists for her. It is often the case that this sequence identification involves school and school friends' behaviour at first. It is rare to begin the process with the behaviour of the child herself in the home. That said, the aim of the life story therapist is to encourage that spotlight on sequencing to be shone into the family home. It is there that the therapist can begin to work alongside the carer and the child to identify behaviour that might be harmful to the child, to the carers, or to other vulnerable people or animals. As the child makes sense of her history, her feelings and her reactive and learnt response behaviours, she is able to adopt change and feel the positive effects of doing so.

Internalization ends once the child has reached her current state. We then engage in review and, for some, a physical journey helps to capture memories and create a direct sensory link with the past. This journey does not include visits to people from the past, just the environment and important landmarks in the child's life. I remember taking a child on a life journey to the Lake District area of the UK. We arrived at his previous school and he recalled the hills and the landmarks and then told us about the den he used to have and asked if he could see if it was still there. It was, and so we took pictures of this for his book. This boy's father had committed suicide, and we had spent a lot of time talking about him on the wallpaper. We went to the Sellafield nuclear power station in Cumbria, and this boy was fascinated that his father had worked there. We went in and did a tour of the facility and he asked to take pictures and a brochure home. His life story book contains a lovely picture of his father, and behind it we had placed a picture of the plant where his father had worked and the canteen where his parents had met.

Making the internalization phase as explorative and as interesting as possible will often end in a very detailed life journey, full of thoughts based on fact, fiction, fantasy and the actions of others.

3. Third stage: Life story book

The life story book itself is the third stage, and this is typically presented as the evidence of the work being achieved.

The book contains the information recorded on the wallpaper, which has now been internalized by the child. Children who have engaged in this process are able to decide what they have in the book as a representation for others to see, whereas the work that is completed in the direct sessions can be stored confidentially and remain within the second stage process.

> It is generally accepted that life story books should answer the what, when and why questions about a child's life experiences. They should also be used as a means to allow the child, without undue pressure, to express feelings about these events. Life [story] work is a means of unravelling confusion and discarding some of the negative emotional baggage which the child has carried for so long. (Connor *et al.*, 1985)

The book itself is used as a celebration to mark the occasion that the work has concluded. The use of the book in the later life of the child should prove valuable and a source of comfort. I am aware of many uses for a quality life story engagement; these include introduction to new placements, memory and confirmation of self, explanation of the past to loved ones, and a validation for others of the life that has been led.

Life story therapy in practice

Case study: Britney

Britney is a 14-year-old child who was subject to a series of sexual assaults by her birth mother when she was an infant. Following a police and social service investigation she was removed from her mother and placed with her grandparents, first under a care order and then under an agreed residence order (both within the Children Act 1989).

Despite all the support of her grandparents, Britney was beginning to struggle with the memory of what her mother had done, and this was seeping into her school life. She had recently moved from a school in the local area and attended a busy secondary school, where she was fortunate to have access to a project run within the school aiming to help children identified as struggling with engagement with education, and support for herself overseen by Maxine E, a family worker for the school.

I was asked to consider working with Britney and help her to manage her behaviour and feelings around the school. This was agreed, as long as the school provided a safe place to work, attendance by Maxine at therapy sessions, and the creation of a recovery team around Britney. In order for the story book to be successful, I also set up meetings with Britney's grandparents to engage their permission and support for the work.

When Britney first met me, I explained the idea of the story work and acknowledged with her that the work would only include her thoughts, feelings and memories, would only follow where she wished to go, and would remain confidential as long as the information did not affect the safety and wellbeing of her and other children. We began the work in January 2010 and concluded in July 2011. (This included a five-month break, as Britney decided that she had done enough at the time.) Her story work was subject to confrontation, examination and an invitation for her to attach feelings and emotions to the events illustrated.

Using the methods of life story therapy on areas of her life that she wished to explore, Britney was able to make sense of her internal and external worlds. This culminated in a detailed child protection statement to the police and the ultimate protection of her younger sister, who was consequently made subject to care proceedings on her mother's arrest. Within the story work approach, Britney was also able to make sense of her story without the interference of the stories of others. At the conclusion of the work, Britney was back in full-time education. She was selected to attend a group for gifted and talented students, as a result of which she has begun day release at a local university. Her placement with the grandparents, which had always been fraught with uncertainty, mistrust and confusion, was recovered, and Britney's future now looks much more positive.

With the permission of Britney and Maxine, I include their feedback as to the experience of this approach and how it has impacted on them.

Maxine's summary

This work has been instrumental in helping a 14-year-old girl understand and work through some very disturbing events from her childhood.

Britney transferred to her present school from another secondary school in December 2008. She had moved because she alleged that staff and pupils at the school had targeted her. There was no information given to the present school about her background, other than that she has lived with her maternal grandparents since she was six years of age.

Britney found it hard to settle and was challenging, defiant and uncooperative. She spent most of her time interfering in other pupils' problems and used school time for social interaction. She was hospitalised from school on one occasion after taking an overdose of paracetamol. However, despite attempts to support her, her challenging behaviour continued. She was referred to me after becoming distressed and upset in school and had started to share personal information with school staff. She was not eating well and presented as a very sad child. There had been referrals to the Child and Adolescent Mental Health Service regarding her emotional welfare.

Although this work has taken more than 12 months, there have been breaks. Britney was enthusiastic about the story work and spoke about her feelings and how she found certain things very difficult to talk or think about. She is a very astute child and wanted to know about her mother and her mother's past. She was aware of the incestuous behaviour of her great-grandfather, but she was too angry at times to tolerate the impact such events consequently had upon her.

The therapy work was stopped at Britney's request once it had covered the areas of concern that she had identified, but in January 2011 I contacted Richard [the author] again and asked that we re-engage. Britney was tearful, anxious and frightened, as she had thought about her mother and her mother's actions towards her. This led to a police interview and care proceedings for extended family members, and all through this time Britney relied upon the meetings at the school. Story work continued throughout this time and she was able to speak freely about her mother, her home life, and difficulties with her grandparents and her relationships at the school.

Her attendance at school has improved, as she began to engage in lessons and making contributions to school life. She is seen as a potential high achiever within the school and has recently been selected to attend the gifted and talented students' course at a local university.

It is clear that, without the life story therapy, she would not have had the opportunity to work through this very complex story in such depth in a safe, supported environment. Who knows where the future will take her, but she is now on the way, although there is more for her to achieve.

From my perspective, life story therapy should be available to some, not all, of our troubled, challenging pupils who express themselves through personally destructive behaviours and anger, which is a great barrier to learning and reaching their full potential. Often troubled young people have not had the opportunity to tell their story and work through the process of grief, acceptance and understanding in a safe and supportive environment.

Britney's conclusion

I started life story therapy 12 months ago and at first I didn't think it would help me at all. As time passed, each few weeks I felt that Richard and Maxine understood me more and more. The simplest of things we used to do with the wallpaper and how Richard helped me understand things helped me more and more. Things got easier and I began to understand myself for the first time. Without life story therapy, I would still have been misbehaving in school and not being able to express my feelings and understand what was making me behave the way I was. It has helped me so much and changed my life.

Chapter 2

The Developing Brain, the Body, Trauma and Attachment

Life story therapists engage with the child, and in doing so, the therapist engages with the child's brain. It is essential to understand the development of the brain and its function and chemistry. Technology continues to provide more and more insight as a result of discoveries about the architecture of the brain, its individual blueprint and its susceptibility to the environment within which it has developed. It has become evident that exposure to trauma leaves its mark on the brain's ability to reach its full potential. It is through continuing technological breakthroughs that therapists will be able to identify, apply and asses interventions that will support the child's recovery.

> Understanding of the rudiments of human brain function and brain development can provide very useful and practical insight to the, all-too-often, puzzling emotional, behavioral, cognitive, social and physical problems that the interdisciplinary team faces when working with maltreated children. (Perry 1996)

This chapter will provide a brief introduction to the brain, its development and environmental shaping, drawing on current research at Harvard University, Child Trauma Academy Houston and various other sources that are uncovering the secrets of the brain.

Bessel Van der Kolk and Pat Ogden have contributed to our understanding of the importance of the body and how the body is affected by trauma, both in its memory and in its adaption to physical experiences. Van der Kolk's seminal work *The Body Keeps the Score* (1994) is an excellent reference for the trauma experience and for how intervention which cares for the body is as health-giving and therapeutic in its effect as cognitive therapy in addressing the brain. Ogden (with Kekuni Minton) wrote an article called 'Sensorimotor sequencing: One method for processing traumatic memory' (2000), which identifies the link between body movement and what is being experienced at the sensory level at times of trauma, and supports the individual to work with the body and senses rather than working only on the cognitive memory of the trauma.

Trauma and attachment is a key area for life story therapy, and this chapter considers definitions of trauma and its potential consequences for the brain, the body, and the human need for positive and healthy attachment. Attachment is essential for the healthy development of the child and the emerging adult.

> Children with attachment disorder have often been victims of abuse, neglect and multiple separations/disruptions. Their trauma, fear, anxiety and painful emotions are lodged in the primitive portion of their brains. (Levy 2010)

The developing brain

> ...an awareness of human brain development and functioning provides practical insights into the origins of the abnormal functioning seen following adverse developmental experiences (e.g. abuse, neglect and trauma) and furthermore, [that] an understanding of how neural systems change suggests specific therapeutic interventions. (Perry 2006)

The brain begins to form when the foetus is three weeks old. Within two months the foetus begins to make sense of its environment within and without the womb. The dramatic growth of the brain is due to the development of the 'circuitry' of the brain through the neural processes and synapse connections (see Figure 2.1) which form the essential pathways.

The brain and the nervous system are made up of cells; one type of nerve cell is the neuron. Neurons consist of three sections: the cell body, dendrites and axons (see below).

The brain begins to produce neurons during the prenatal phase, and these neurons migrate to sensitive parts of the brain in order to perform specialized actions. Described as the 'building blocks' of the nervous system, there are three types of neurons in the human body: the sensory, the motor and the inter neurons. *Sensory* neurons are responsible for converting external stimuli into electric pulses. They are specialized to communicate information gained from the environment through the senses of light, sound and temperature. *Motor* neurons originate in the spinal cord, and their axons communicate beyond the central nervous system, i.e. they communicate information to muscles and glands. *Inter* neurons represent the largest group of neurons within the body and transmit information between neurons.

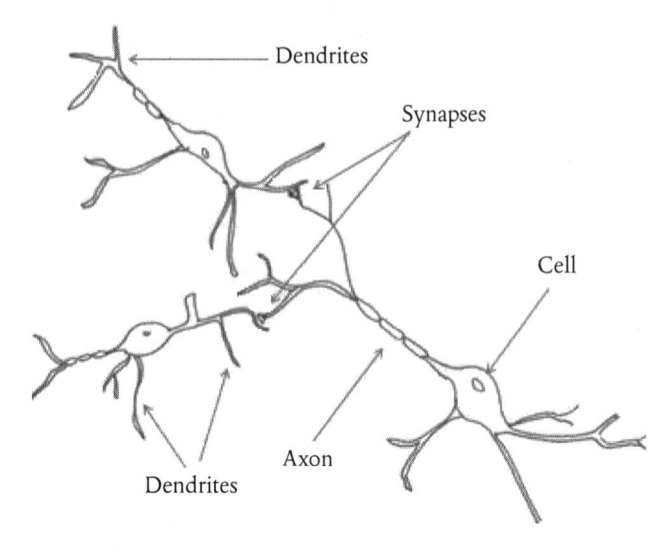

Figure 2.1 Three nerve cells (neurons)

The neuron structure may be covered with a substance called myelin, a white-coloured, fatty substance that protects the axon, in sections separated by nodes. The myelin acts as a boost for the signals sent and received between the axon and dendrites, as well as providing insulation. Myelin-covered neurons are often referred to as white matter whereas areas of the neurons (nodes) and other neurons not covered with myelin are referred to as grey matter. Neurons communicate by sending electronic 'messages' along the axon and receive electronic pulses 'messages' through the dendrites.

Neurons are not physically connected: there are microscopic gaps called 'synapses' between the dendrites of adjacent neurons. Via its dendrites, each neuron can connect across synapse gaps to more than 15,000 other neurons, which together create the architecture of the brain. The synapse itself is in three parts: the presynaptic ending, the synaptic cleft and the postsynaptic ending. The presynaptic ending contains the neurotransmitter; the cleft is the 'gap' that the messages cross; and the postsynaptic ending is the point at which the 'action potential' occurs.

Neurotransmitters are a group of chemicals in the brain that facilitate communication between the neurons. Neurotransmitters travel across the synapse gap and convey messages across the cells in the brain. The 'firing' of the chemical and electronic pulse within the neuron is not guaranteed: there may be both connection and action, or not. Therefore the action potential is based on an 'all or none' law:

> The all-or-none law guarantees that once an action potential is generated it is always full size, minimizing the possibility that information will be lost along the way. (Levitan and Kaczmarik 1991)

At birth, the average baby brain weighs approximately 300 grams. This represents about 10 per cent of the baby's body weight, the baby brain is 20 per cent of the average adult brain weight, whereas the adult brain, weighing approximately 1,400 grams, is about 2 per cent of adult body weight. A healthy baby will be born with the ability to see, touch, hear, smell and taste. Two-thirds of the brain architecture is present at birth In its structure and anatomy, the newborn baby's brain is remarkably like that of an adult. The major difference between the baby and the adult brain is in the number of synapses between the 100 billion nerve cells, some of which have already developed in the infant brain, and many more that have not.

Huttenlocher (1991) set out to count synapses within the forming brain. He performed autopsies on brains ranging from the foetus stage to those of people in their 90s. He found that a 28-week foetus had 124 million synapses, a newborn 253 million.

The synapses present at birth are found in the primary regions of the brain which govern areas such as breathing, eating and sleeping. From birth the brain rapidly begins to organize, as synapses form to create pathways:

> At its peak, the cerebral cortex of a healthy toddler may create 2 million synapses per second. (Zero to Three 2009)

It is believed that at three years of age children have more than 1000 trillion synapses, which are more than the child requires, and over the next ten years these will be 'pruned' and become dormant. By the time the child is 13 years old, these connections will have been reduced to less than 500 trillion, and will remain so for most of her life (Ackerman 2007).

The elasticity of the brain affords new learning, pruning and shaping, and the brain evolves depending upon how it is used – the idea of 'use it or lose it'. The brain continues to develop throughout the life of the child and throughout her adulthood until death, but neurons do not reproduce:

those present at birth are the totality that the individual produces, and gradually they die and are not replaced. Instead the brain is able to wire and rewire with the neurons that are available, adapting to change, whether internal or external.

The organizing process of the brain is achieved through memory, hence the importance that clinicians such as Dispensa (2008) and Perry (2004) emphasize in respect of repetition, repetition and repetition: neurons in the brain encode repeated events, and soon the smoothing of the neuron pathway creates memory.

The more frequently a certain pattern of neural activation occurs, the more indelible the internal representation – the more indelible the 'memory'. (Perry 1997)

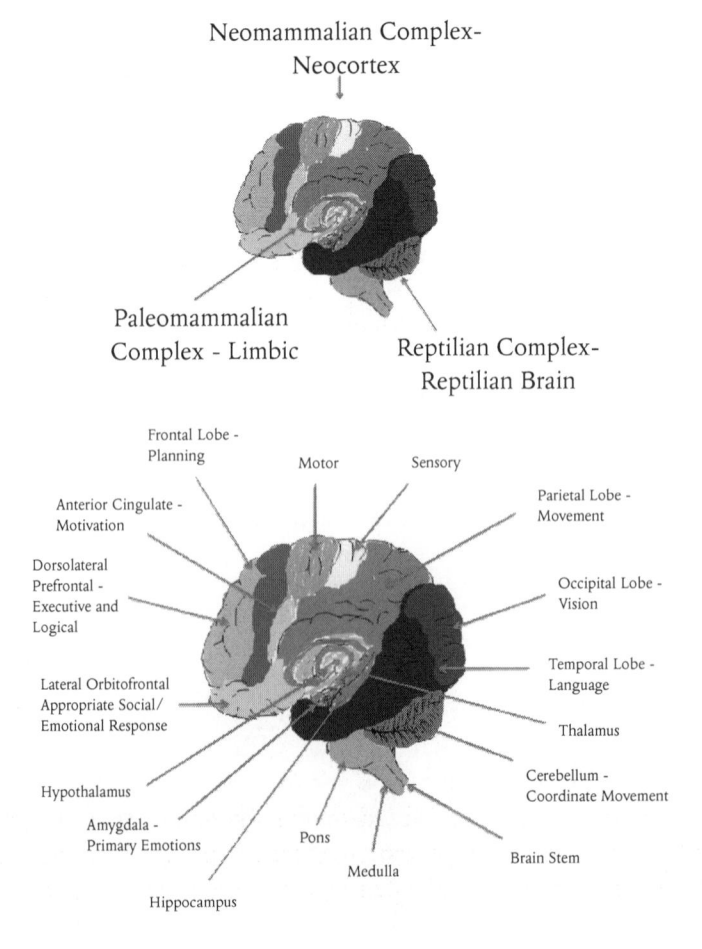

Figure 2.2 Illustration of the brain and functions

Embryologically, the human brain is an extension of the spinal cord, and through the experience of evolution, the brain has developed and grown, and is now three times the size of the brain of our ancestor 'homo erectus' (Smithsonian 2007). As the human species experienced the difficulties of the environment, primarily to achieve survival, the brain evolved to recognize threat.

MacLean (1985) introduced the notion of the 'triune brain', three separate brains which are independent of each other, but designed to work together:

1. The reptilian brain is the lower brain, and is the oldest part of the brain. It consists of the structures of the brain stem: the medulla, the pons, the cerebellum and the mesencephalon, the globus pallidus and the olfactory bulbs.

- The *medulla oblongata* controls autonomic systems. As motor and sensory neurons from other regions of the brain travel through the medulla, the medulla transmits messages to the brain and the spinal cord to ensure that such functions as breathing, swallowing, heart and digestive actions are maintained.

- The *pons* connects the cerebral cortex with the medulla and serves as a bridge between the two hemispheres of the brain, coordinating and transferring messages between and beyond other parts of the brain and the spinal cord.

- The *cerebellum* is responsible for the coordination of balance and movement and has a folded surface area which affords it the opportunity to hold and process large quantities of information. The *mesencephalon* controls vision-related functions including eye movement and pupil dilation, and controls movement through sight.

- The *globus pallidus* works in harmony with the cerebellum so that the movement of the human is smooth and balanced.

- The *olfactory bulbs* are responsible for smell, transmitting messages from the nose to the brain. They can discriminate among odours, and filter out odours so as to transmit information required for higher brain functions.

All these regions are fundamental to the autonomic nervous system (breathing, sleeping and digestion). In some animals the brain stem and cerebellum dominate, but in the human, the development of higher brain functions challenge, in the main successfully for authority. The reptilian brain is rigid, set, and repeats behaviours regardless of the outcome of such behaviours.

2. The paleomammalian brain, or limbic system (MacLean 1952), is the middle brain and comprises the amygdala, hippocampus, thalamus and the hypothalamus.

- The *amygdala* plays a key role in the way memories are internalized and stored in the brain, which is thought to be based on an event's sensory and emotional effect.
- The *hippocampus* seeks to filter and, when required, send memories to the cerebral hemisphere for storage, but can retrieve these from the storage regions when needed.
- The *hypothalamus*, although small in comparison to the other parts of the limbic system, regulates body temperature, hormones and glands.
- The *thalamus* connects areas of the cerebral cortex with the spinal cord and other regions of the brain in order to assist sensory perception and movement.

3. The neomammalian brain, the cerebrum, comprises almost the whole of the right and left hemispheres, the neocortex. This 'brain' constitutes almost two-thirds of total brain mass.

Maclean undertook much of his research on small animals such as hamsters and mice; in a series of experiments he removed parts of the brain from such animals and noted that the animal concerned was then unable to complete certain tasks such as play and nurturing, but in all other areas they were able to perform adequately. He hypothesized that to do the same to a human subject would result in the human becoming little more than a 'vegetable'.

Since 1980 the basic knowledge of brain structure, function and the effects of early life trauma have been vastly expanded by the work of Schore, Perry and other notable contributors.

Schore (1997) states that the shape of the person we become is forged by our interactions with the environment that surrounds us. The subsequent growth of the brain is therefore directly affected by the stimulation that causes it to react and to be active.

> A major conclusion of the last decade of developmental neuroscience research is that there is now agreement that the

infant brain 'is designed to be moulded by the environment it encounters' (Thomas *et al.* 1997)

When the child is held and hugged, brain networks are activated and strengthened and firing spreads to associated networks; when the child is sung to, still other networks are strengthened to receive sounds and interpret them as song. The repeated appearance of the mother provides a fixation object, as in imprinting. (Schore 2005)

Baby brains develop sequentially – as Perry (2003) describes, 'from bottom to top'. They respond automatically to sensorimotor cues, and such responses may override their cognitive capacity. Such unregulated responses may be destructive to the self and others, while engaging the most primitive survival needs.

Huge portions of the human brain are devoted to social functions and communication including establishing and maintaining eye contact, reading faces, judgments and more. When a baby is born, his brain houses over one hundred billion neurons that will chart paths and make connections based on the social experiences they encounter. By the age of two and a half, approximately 85 percent of the baby's neurological growth is complete; meaning the foundation of their brain's capacity is in place. By age three, the child's brain is 90 percent of its completed adult size. (Perry 2007)

With ever increasing exploration of the brain and our understanding of its potential, it is now possible to take images of the brain as it develops and observe the state of the brain and its growth, where it is 'lit' up and where development is not as healthy.

There is a growing body of evidence which suggests that psychological trauma has a powerful influence on the development of the brain. The effects of abuse on the person are an attack on the brain, whether the abuse is physical, emotional, neglectful, sexual or a combination of all or some of these forms.

Bremner (1999) considered the effects of abuse on memory, in particular in the hippocampus.

Once viewed as genetically programmed, the brain is now known to be plastic, an organ moulded by both genes and experience throughout life. A single traumatic experience can alter an adult's brain: A horrifying battle, for instance, may induce the flashbacks, depression and hair-trigger response of post-traumatic stress disorder (PTSD). And researchers are finding that abuse and neglect early in life can have even more devastating consequences, tangling both the chemistry and the architecture of children's brains and leaving them at risk for drug abuse, teen pregnancy and psychiatric problems later in life. (Brownlee 1996)

The effect of her environment on the child, whether healthy and nurturing or unhealthy and neglectful, is to shape the brain and the memory within. Studies by Chamberlain (1989) showed that babies and young children require the experience of stable and predictable attachments which are of a warm and loving nature. He found that in children and babies who did not experience positive interactions, brain development which promotes development in caring behaviour and cognition was impaired.

Our brains are sculpted by our early experiences. Maltreatment is a chisel that shapes a brain to contend with strife, but at the cost of deep, enduring wounds. (Teicher 2000a)

Readers interested in the brain and its infrastructure will be well rewarded if they log onto Bruce Perry's website located within the pages of www.childtrauma.org. There are excellent and informative works by Allan Schore around affect regulation and the left/right brain on www.allanschore.com. Work in progress in the Centre for the Developing Child at Harvard University is also well worth a visit, at www.developingchild.harvard.edu.

The body

There is resurgence in the study of the body and how memories are held within it. Triggers, often nonverbal, may cause a physical reaction which is automatic and not associated with cognitive storytelling. Addressing trauma through talking and narrative work cannot successfully cure the somatic aspects of trauma. Van der Kolk (1992) argues that trauma therapy has to involve the individual in working with their 'body states'. A core component of this approach is the individual's ability to 'calm'.

Levine (1997) argues that trauma is a biological response to a perceived and/or actual threat, where the body is unable to discharge the experience physically and therefore the experience is locked within.

This is reminiscent of Kardiner's (Kardiner and Spiegel 1947) 'memory boxes': the memory (often referred to as 'procedural memory') is held within the body. Kardiner identified that the body of wounded and traumatized soldiers become their 'memory' box, the body holds what has been experienced and it is this memory, held fast and weighted which can trouble the future health and wellbeing of the person. Children who are traumatized by the experience of violent acts (whether as a direct or non-direct occurrence) store the memory, the reactions, the thoughts and the feelings. In effect their bodies, as well as their brain, become a storage facility of memory – a 'person-sized memory box'.

Traumatized children are often stuck in this state, unable to dissipate the energy and the arousal, and as a result are left preoccupied with their experiences. It is within this state that normal function and healthy development of children is difficult if not impossible. In order to provide a therapeutic response, the individual is helped to regain biological control by reworking the trauma and completing the action.

> It's via the awareness of deep bodily experience that people can begin to move around the way that they feel – not by keeping it out there…the story of what happened is worth telling, but to change your reaction to it, you have to go via the deep internal felt sense. (Pointon 2004)

The body learns to respond, and, although controlled by the brain, the response mechanism and muscle memory are triggered before the instigator is assessed as a current rather than a past threat. A child who has an internal working model which tells them that she is worthless, incompetent and therefore defenceless, will have hyper-vigilant tendencies. If she feels on edge, susceptible to continual attack, and wary of all new and current engagements, her body is affected by a 'state of readiness' which ultimately affects its presentation and health. In a reality of threats, the somatic senses and response to trauma influence the body's relationship with the environment, and therefore the subsequent action taken is not selective but reactive to the expectation of harm.

The physical changes adopted by the body in certain situations can become 'instinctive' and 'memorized' (such as defensive actions). The child may raise an arm to protect herself from a perceived risk, but aligned with the raising of her arm, she will regulate herself to the threat perceived, so activating her autonomic nervous system, and with it, breathing and muscle movement.

Traumatized children may have dysregulated emotional systems, which in turn may cause miscommunication between the brain structures:

> ...a history of neglect, physical and/or sexual abuse, multiple maltreatment subtypes, and earlier onset of maltreatment was directly related to symptoms of emotion dysregulation. Symptoms of emotion dysregulation are also at the core of a construct called Developmental Trauma Disorder, a diagnosis intended to be used in children and adolescents reflecting the complex adaptations to prolonged psychological trauma in childhood. (Van der Kolk and d'Andrea 2010)

A certain movement by an individual may trigger a response to a memory of danger. This may then trigger an escalation in the response activated by the past memory, which can then turn to a survival response (fight, flight or freeze). These automatic response issues can override all attempts to 'reason' the response through the activation of the whole brain, and the initial message received by the reptilian brain may be interpreted as so overwhelming that further thought is impossible.

Body movement includes instinctive and directive, conscious and unconscious elements, so that the child may or may not be in control of physical response processes such as aggression and self-harm activities. She may abscond (run away), not settle, create chaos; or she may engage in frozen watchfulness. Some children may wet and/or soil their beds or their clothes, hide soiled clothes and faeces in places such as drawers – yet, when challenged, they do not realize or understand why, when or what were the reasons for doing so. In my experience with children who have such behaviours, their carers often become frustrated, angry and dismissive of the actions because the child cannot explain them. Traumatized children carry their trauma with them, and survival shapes their conscience and decision making. In the bottom-up process, their survival need may override any other options that could 'balance' their instinctive action.

A few years ago I was involved in a car accident. Fortunately I was not too badly affected, but now, when I sense the risk of a similar incident, my arm involuntarily springs into action as I hold my passenger back in their seat, anticipating the 'crash'. This movement is the result of a memory process, where I have responded to the perceived threat, despite the absence of such an incident occurring.

Body movement involves all forms of physical and biological change, from gross and fine motor movements to physiological change within the internal organs, the pulse and nerves, and these 'somatic markers' influence the decision making that guides response to harm. Antonio Damasio (1999) introduces an excellent example of the use of somatic markers. (Consider how a child who has witnessed a violent act between her parents experiences the external environment and registers this.)

> Essentially, objects in the external environment cause patterns of activation of retinal receptive cells, and these retinal patterns are processed serially and in parallel to extract the visual aspects of the environment that we perceive. Patterns in the external world correspond with patterns of nerve cell activity in the brain, and these brain patterns are termed *cognitive representations*. So 'thinking' is done by means of patterns of nerve cell activation. (Charlton 2000)

Damasio suggests that the brain is able store these representations in its working memory. The next time the external environment presents similar stimuli, the working memory remembers the body state and so projects this.

The sensory information is gathered and stored and at the same time the child is aware of her internal emotional environment, how she has reacted to the visual and sound effects. She is then able to combine the two parts and 'learn' through the process of 'cognitive representation' which identifies the external and the internal relationship.

As with the formation of internal working models, the early relationships that we enjoy with our primary carer will shape how we use our bodies to engage, to communicate and move within close contact. We literally shape ourselves to the environment that surrounds us. If we are loved, supported and encouraged, our bodies become cared for, supported and strong in posture, structure and purpose. If the opposite is true, the body becomes unloved, unsupported and purposeless, therefore uncared for, unsupported and weak. Often, when I meet children for the first time, their bodies tell me the sadness of their experience and the enormity of the burden they carry.

Pat Ogden and Kekuni Minton (2000) wrote an article called 'Sensorimotor sequencing: One method for processing traumatic memory' which accepts the premise that:

> Traumatized individuals are plagued by the return of dissociated, incomplete or ineffective sensorimotor reactions in such forms as intrusive images, sounds, smells, body sensations, physical pain, constriction, numbing and the inability to modulate arousal. (Ogden and Minton 2000)

They discuss the process of supporting the individual to consider the trauma episodes. As the body reacts to the memory, the individual is asked to focus on her body sensations and learn to understand these cognitively and then to go on to master this reaction. The two central pillars of sensorimotor psychotherapy are the therapeutic relationship (supporting awareness of the sensory state and how to regulate this healthily) and education of the individual to independently regulate her sensorimotor process by contacting the part of her body that is troubling her, tracking her concerns and her trauma and articulating the feelings associated with this:

> Sensorimotor Psychotherapy provides clients with tools to deal with disturbing bodily reactions, and they frequently report feeling increasingly safe as they begin to learn how to limit the amount of information they must process at any given moment by focusing attention on sensation. (Ogden and Minton 2000)

Trauma

Life story therapy is all about the shards of lives which have been, in the cases of multi-placed children, cast aside during their life course. We are all left with these shards, often painful, incomplete and jarring against the new contacts that we engage with as we develop.

When we work with children who have challenges, our main focus is to help them achieve better outcomes, to protect them and to make them feel better. We all have challenges, some big and some small, and sometimes the easiest response is to solve the problem quickly and hope that it is dealt with – but the pitfall of this approach is often that the root cause of the challenge has not been understood – that, like an iceberg of which only the tip is seen, the visible issue is addressed but the underlying danger still exists. Presenting problems often contain trauma as the deep-seated reality of the challenge, but this is often hidden and avoided due to the painful issues involved. Often children and adults have a sensitive reaction to certain events. These events, when they take place, cause reactions such as pain, confusion, anger and sadness. Often this is as a result of traumatic memories which have been left unresolved, and are 'weak spots' inside us. At moments of stress, or perceived danger, our response is based on our past experiences.

> Anything that disrupts the optimal development of a child can be defined as a type of trauma to the system. (Ziegler 2002)

There are many examples of trauma response behaviours, and the most often quoted are the responses of 'flight, fight or freeze'. A child who has experienced persistent violence from her father when he returns from the pub will register a smell, and when that smell is perceived again, the child (who may now be an adult) will react. This reaction could be a memory, an action or a response that can be automatic. What is referred to as a 'coping style' is often based on reactions that are tried and trusted and dependent on immediacy, rather than a thought-out response.

Assessing the impact on the development of a child who has been traumatized by extraordinary events is not an exact science; some children become very damaged through experiences of neglect, emotional deprivation, or physical and sexual abuse, while others are able to call on their reserves, to cope with these events (to be more resilient); we are all unique. However, the effects of persistent or critical trauma are costly and, depending on the development of the person traumatized, the cost can be life-consuming.

As an example, a child who has experienced poor care, life-threatening actions and/or rejection at a young age may develop an impaired understanding of herself, her carers and the world in general. These beliefs can be deep-seated and act as the default concept for the rest of the child's life. The traumatized state is a potentially lifelong condition which is linked to learned behaviour (Bandura 1977) reinforced by the experience of repeated trauma. If a child has experienced recurrent criticism, and the message is strong, persistent and consistent, then the child will own this and memorize that she is bad. The brain learns through reinforcement of action: the more frequent the action, the firmer the learning that is enforced.

If trauma is constant, and threat perceived as real and dangerous, the brain utilizes what resources it can to provide a response that protects the whole. This constant, heightened response involves the child concentrating on the threat and her perceptions of it; however, the brain has already selected where it is required to respond, and this means that healthy development in the brain is not underway. Important learning does not take place, as the brain is on guard and the trauma has become the focus of learning.

> Bottom-up processing takes precedence in times of emergency, when it is advantageous to short-circuit the cortex and activate a motor-pattern generated directly from the brain stem. If we suddenly see a car careening toward us, we instantly turn our car away; we react automatically, and only later (even if it is only a split second later) do we realize there is danger and feel afraid. (Hobson 1994)

Schore (1997) states that in trauma the brain, far from being inactive, is active in areas of priority. Priority relates to the fear response, which in turn creates permanent 'memories' that shape flight and fight responses within their environment. Less well formed are the areas of learning which require the brain to be calm (often referred to as 'attentive calm').

> Hard-wired to be governed by somatic and emotional states, infants respond automatically to sensorimotor and affective cues and to the mercy of their sensations, physical reactions and emotions, having lost the capacity to regulate these functions. (Schore 1994)

Trauma (shell shock) during World War I, in particular, led to study of the brain and the effects of shock. When people are traumatized, it has been said that they have experienced 'speechless terror', where the experience has left them unable to make verbal sense of what has occurred, but they retain an indelible memory of pictures, smell, touch, taste and sound.

With the capacity to 'make sense' of the experience under attack, those who are traumatized lose their ability to utilize their emotions as positive guides. They may be unable to organize thoughts and feelings, becoming detached in order to cope. This disassociation from the present can present as disinterest, empty of empathy and/or emotion. With the children (and adults) I work with, this emotional incapacity can be evident in the unpredictable responses and behaviours on show. Children can be angry, submissive, confrontational or passively agreeable. Trauma is a heavy burden, and many children who I work with are unsure how to relieve the weight they carry. The majority have experienced incredible trauma at a preverbal age, and their ability to make sense of the actions visited on them is at even more of a disadvantage. In life story therapy, the trauma that we visit may not have been processed by the child, and may still be contained within her. As she reaches a realization, she may become vulnerable. The danger of retraumatizing is at its highest at these times, and so the ability of the life story therapist, and the knowledge he has of the child, must be equal to the risk.

Perry (2006) introduced his approach to working with traumatized children through an approach called the Neurosequential Model. The Child Trauma Academy (www.childtrauma.org).

> An essential component of Dr Perry's Neurosequential Model of Therapeutics is the assessment of each child's unique brain functioning. The child's treatment team works together to assess the level of development in four core areas of the brain including the brain stem, diencephalon, limbic, and cortex... This information is entered into Dr Perry's metric program and a brain map is generated. The team then interprets the results of the brain map in order to identify interventions that are essential to the therapeutic process. (Alexander Youth Network 2011)

The model is not a therapeutic process in itself, but a neurobiological approach to assist in informing the clinical practice team working with the child. The model is based on a 'brain map'; the clinician refers to the mapping of functional areas of the brain to assist in timing, initial delivery and continued use of therapeutic intervention, in order to support the traumatized child towards a healthier developmental trajectory.

There are three stages that the diagnostic tool identifies within the programme. The first is to understand the history of the child (where the child has been):

> In order to understand an individual one needs to know his or her history. (Perry and Hambrick 2008)

The second stage is to understand the child's current brain function; this is achieved by a professional team considering the evidence and the current presentation of the child, using the 'brain map' which locates the developed, developing and underdeveloped areas (where the child is). The 'brain map' is made up of 32 sections, each of which attracts a numerical score between 1 and 12: 18 sections in the cortex region, 8 in the limbic and 6 in the diencephalon and brain stem. (More detail can be obtained from the Child Trauma Academy website, www.childtrauma.

org. The programme itself stems from Dr Bruce Perry's team at the Child Trauma Academy in Houston, Texas, USA, and is taught as a programme of intervention as the Neurosequential Model of Therapeutic Care.)

The third stage of the model is the planning and action stage, which requires clear recommendations for therapeutic interventions such as direct or non-direct therapy, reflexology, music and massage, leading to play, art and then to cognitive interventions such as narrative, behavioural and life story therapy. The 'brain map' is then considered regularly to identify change and to continue, alter or stop particular interventions.

Attachment

> The heart of the family is the mother because life comes from her. (Onondaga People, Onondaga County, New York)

Neurophysiology has enlightened us regarding the impact of trauma and health on the brain, and how the brain is structured as the developing child receives and perceives the care she is given. Children attain an understanding of the self, their place in the world and how they expect carers to be. This is often referred to as the 'internal working model' (Bowlby 1969) and is based on the child's attachment experience with primary carers. The child will develop a belief about herself, those who have care of her and the world in general. A child who has a positive internal working model feels that she is competent, worthwhile and lovable; that her carers are kind, caring, protective and loving; and that the world is a safe place which has a space for her. Children who lack positive experiences may develop the belief that they are helpless, worthless and unlovable; that their carers are hurtful, uncaring and dislike them; and that the world in general is a scary and unwelcoming place that does not have a place for them (Levy and Orlans 1998)

> These early attachment experiences become internalised as core beliefs and anticipatory images that influence later perceptions, emotions and reactions to others. (Levy and Orlans 1998)

In terms of attachment, children's adaptation to their internal working model can be:

- secure attachment (the carer is loving and the child is loved)

- ambivalence (the caregiver is inconsistent in how he responds and the child sees herself as dependent and poorly valued)
- avoidant (the caregiver is seen as consistently rejecting and the child is insecure but compulsively self-reliant)
- disorganized (caregivers are seen as frightening or frightened, and the child is helpless, or angry and controlling).

(Howe 2000)

Internal working models have been referred to by Archer (2003) as 'road maps' that provide the child with an internal framework of his world, which Perry (1999a) calls 'experience-dependent'.

> IWMs [internal working models] reflect the child's view of, and confidence in, the attachment figures' capacity to provide a safe and caring environment. Moreover, these models, in turn, organise the child's thoughts, memories and feelings regarding attachment figures. Inevitably, they will also act as guides and predictors of future behaviour for the child and analogous attachment figures, such as adoptive parents. (Burnell with Archer 2003)

Schore (1994) describes these models as being burned into the unconscious at the neurobiological level, and Solomon and George (1996) say that, once established, they are highly resistant to change when they experience different care presentation.

> The right brain stores internal working models of the attachment relationship. It processes emotional social information – its functions are as diverse as enabling empathy, humour, and many of the capacities that are fundamental to human subjectivity. (Schore and Carroll 2001)

During the World War II children from the inner cities of the UK were evacuated to families and carers in rural areas of the country. Some children were able to cope with this change but others struggled, and this latter issue became of interest to leading adult psychoanalysts such as Anna Freud (1966), John Bowlby and Donald Winnicott. The concept of attachment and the effects of separation of mother and baby became popular among psychologists, and with the observational theories of these commentators therapeutic child care was introduced by Barbara Docker-Drysdale in 1947 at the Mulberry Bush School for troubled children.

Politicians are often wary of being seen to side with troubled young people – in the UK the Conservative Party leader David Cameron attracted a great deal of attention when he urged citizens to 'hug a hoodie' (referring to the hooded sweaters which young people commonly wear) – yet the entire concept of therapeutic child care and attachment theory was based on Docker-Drysdale's call for society to do exactly the same. David Cameron in his speech:

> Because if you knew that that girl had suffered years of abuse and neglect from her family, and years of institutional indifference from the social services you would begin to understand that there is more to life on the streets than simple crime and simple punishment… So when you see a child walking down the road, hoodie up, head down, moody, swaggering, dominating the pavement – think what has brought that child to that moment. If the police and criminal justice system guard the boundaries of acceptable behaviour – patrolling the territory beyond the pale – then community groups populate the interior. If the police stand for sanctions and penalties, you stand for love. And not a soppy love! I don't see anyone soppy here. But it is about relationships. It is about emotional security. It is about love.

The basis of attachment theory has not altered since the 1940s; rather, the initial foundations have been supported through the work of Mary Ainsworth in the 1960s, Daniel A. Hughes in the 1990s and more recently by Danya Glaser (see Ainsworth 1968, Hughes 1997, Glaser 2006).

In life story therapy, the key aim is to promote an understanding of the child's internal working model, and to work through the experiences of this model in order to identify and 'repair' the damaging effects, and thereby assist the child to reframe her current modus to provide her with a more healthy and life-rewarding model.

In its earliest formulation, attachment theory emphasized the parent–child relationship, and while that relationship remains formative, it is now also known that other relationships throughout our lives impact on our attachment (Pietromonaco and Barrett 2000a, b) Children who have suffered long periods of separation from their parents, or who have lost their parents and suffered severe emotional difficulties, find it extremely difficult to make relationships with others and can become withdrawn. (They can also exhibit various other kinds of behavioural problems.)

In my previous book on life story work, *The Child's Own Story*, I introduced a water-based imagery to help explain the concept of attachment, which is reproduced below. I use this process now for all children over eight years of age, and with all carers, as a basis for explaining life story through attachment.

Imagine that you have three empty water glasses: the first represents the child, the second her parent or primary carer and the third the substitute carer. Put an equal amount of water into each glass, say half full; this water represents the essence of the individuals involved. Hold the glass of the child in your right hand, and the glass of the primary carer in your left hand.

In the third trimester of pregnancy, the baby is developing in the womb and she is reliant on the exchange of certain things from the mother (the primary carer) to ensure that she is healthy. These exchanges include nutrients, blood, sound, touch and emotions. The more consistent, the more repetitive and the more predictable, the more opportunity there is for the baby to become expectant of these exchanges. To illustrate this, exchange water between the two symbolic glasses (making sure that afterwards they both remain half full). Bonding is the physical and psychological connection between the mother and her infant that begins at conception, grows during pregnancy, intensifies at birth and exists forever: all Children are bonded to their biological mothers, regardless of what transpires after birth (Levy and Orlans 2003).

As we are aware, a baby's brain develops an amazing rate and the healthier the messages received, the healthier the baby's growth becomes. (Schore (2001) proposes that the adaptive right brain regulatory capacity is experience-dependent and that the quality of the relationship between the infant and primary carer is crucial to its development.)

At birth the baby is 'hotwired' to relate to her primary carer. As early as 1935, Ian Suttie put forward the view that a child is born to attach to her mother:

> the child is born with a simple attachment-to-mother who is the sole source of food and protection. (Suttie 1935)

The baby relates to the mother, and in a healthy attachment the mother responds. There is an exchange between the baby and the mother for the next 18 months, which includes food, warmth, love, shelter, protection. The baby learns that the mother is caring, protective and loving; she learns that she herself is lovable, worthwhile and competent, and that the world outside this relationship is a welcoming and worthwhile place to be.

One of the most essential experiences in shaping the architecture of the developing brain is 'serve and return' interaction between children and significant adults in their lives. Young children naturally reach out for interaction through babbling, facial expressions and gestures, and adults respond with the same kind of vocalizing and gesturing back at them. This back-and-forth process is fundamental to the wiring of the brain, especially in the earliest years. (Centre for the Developing Child, Harvard University 2011)

In terms of language, a baby who has experienced repetitive engagement with the primary carer in the return 'serve and respond' relationship will learn over 300 more words by the age of two than a child who has not had this level of stimuli (Huttenlocher *et al.* 1991).

To return to the water analogy: as the water is exchanged equally between the two glasses, both mother and child remain healthy. The child has formed a healthy internal working model which will provide her a default stating that she is worthwhile, lovable, loved and cared for, and belongs in the wider world.

> A securely attached child…will have a working model of the world in which she herself is worthy of love and attention, others are expected to be responsive and reliable, and relationships with others are seen as rewarding and fun (Beckett 2002)

Let us return to the third trimester of pregnancy, and consider what can happen if the experience for the child is different. The exchange between the mother and the forming baby may be adversely affected if there are interruptions or missing experiences in the womb. If the health of the mother is affected by drugs and/or alcohol, this may interrupt the exchange of food, the quality of food, the timing of food, and the chemicals that are exchanged may cause harm to the health and development of the baby. The mother may be a victim of domestic violence; as she is harmed, her baby is also. Experiences of extreme fear, stress, emotional imbalance; unexplained sound which is unpredictable and stressful; touch that might be hurtful, unpredictable and stressful; the effects of mental health problems, emotional violence and, sadly, many more impacts, may visit the unborn child.

At birth, the child is 'hotwired' to relate to the mother. Perhaps, as the child attempts to relate, the mother cannot, or does not, respond in kind. As you pour water from the child's glass into the mother's, you will see that the child's glass is beginning to empty as the mother is not responding by refilling it. After a while the child begins to learn that it would be dangerous to continue to give, and so stops. The baby learns that crying does not help – she can continue to cry, but it makes no sense, so the baby stops crying.

> Infants have the genetic predisposition to form strong attachments to their primary caregivers. But if a child's caregivers are unresponsive or threatening, and the attachment process is disrupted, the child's ability to form any healthy relationships during his or her life may be impaired. (Child Welfare Information Gateway 2009)

Now place a 'lid' (use your hand) over the top of the child's glass; this represents the child learning that she cannot afford to continue to give to the parent, as she may not survive if more of her essence is lost. She learns that she must care for herself, and that attachment to someone close is dangerous. In many of our professional fields we see children who no longer live in their family homes and considered that they themselves were responsible for the breakdown.

> Children with grossly neglectful parents…will think of all kinds of excuses for the neglect in order to protect themselves from concluding that their parents do not care about them. They may tell themselves that they deserve the neglect or that they prefer things the way they are. (Beckett 2002)

For children in care, along comes the substitute carer, represented by the third glass. The carer sees the damaged/hurt child and immediately wants to give love and care to the child. They pour from their own glass into the child's, but as the child's glass is covered, the water flows down the side. The child does not receive from the carer, as she has learnt that this might be dangerous. The carer, encouraged by support workers, will continue to try and 'give' to the child, but the child keeps her 'lid' shut. What happens to the carer's glass? It begins to empty, and then the carer realizes that she has little left in her own resource, expresses that the child has drained her, and the placement breaks down. We are left with the child's glass: she no longer has the carer caring for her, she has learnt that she is bad, helpless and unlovable, and twists the lid tighter; she has learnt that the carer is like the first – uncaring, unloving and hurtful; and that the world is not safe and holds no place for her. We are left with a glass which represents a child with a poor 'internal working model'.

This is an evocative exercise and one which has really assisted carers to see that for children, especially multi-placed children, the need they have is not for love alone, but for replication of events missed out on at the beginning of life. When I share this exercise with children, they get it. One child, a 14-year-old, immediately understood the process and stated that he was like the child with the near-empty glass. He explained how he had been let down, and how he felt that it was his fault and that he deserved the difficulties he currently experienced. The question for him and for other children and carers, however, is 'What can we do to support the gentle removal of the lid?'

> Traumatized children will require opportunities to experience attachment relationships which offer consistency, nurture and predictability. Carers can be resourced to understand the significance of daily exchanges in providing the basis for children to develop alternative schema that counteract previous attachment patterns. (Mitchell 2008)

If we consider the messages from the above descriptors of the brain and the body, for trauma and attachment, it is clear that we need to replicate the healthy models from early healthy development. In organizations such as SACCS, the ideal treatment would be to provide safety and containment around the child, to make this clear, consistent and predictable. Healthy attachment is the enduring emotional connection between caregivers and child, characterized by trust, security and the desire for closeness, particularly when the child is under stress (Levy and Orlans 2003).

Creating an environment that is dependable, boundaries that are strong, explained and visible, creates the opportunity for the child to begin to relate with the external world. Going back to the water glasses: take the healthy model – we have the infant and she is content. She will engage in a healthy dance of attachment, and when a new person interacts with her she engages in 'peek-a-boo'. This game is an attachment activity. The infant peeks and you boo; she continues the interplay by hiding behind her attachment figure; as she becomes more confident and receives encouragement from her parent, she instigates 'peek-a-boo' (the 'serve and return' concept). As she becomes more mobile, with age, she will crawl away from the mother, but at a certain distance will turn round and seek assurance from her. If her mother is not attentive, or shows concern, the child will return to her safe place. (Characteristic of attachment is a tendency to seek and maintain proximity to a specific figure, particularly when under stress (Bowlby 1969)).

We need to 'play peek-a-boo' with the children who are affected by insecure attachment issues. The 14-year-old I mentioned above understood that he could peel back his lid when he felt safe, but could put it back when feeling unsafe. He drew the glass on wallpaper and explained that he would like to play 'peek-a-boo' more often.

We need to be present for the child to see that we are attentive and available to her. The idea of the glass and the lid is that the option to open or close the lid is absolutely the child's. It is for the carer to be able to offer safe, secure, consistent and predictable environments for that option to be viable.

Life story is a way in which children can gently learn to play the game, to look, to explore and to hide. We can tell that we are successful, not by the removal of the lid, but by how frequently the lid is opened and how long it remains so. For many of the children I work with, the need to cover their glass is as great as the need to loosen the same. Helping children to recognize when either response is most useful for them increases their ability to recover and cope within the environments in which they reside.

> Bowlby – like Freud – believed that the reason why the attachment was there was that the mother was a regulator of distressed state. As he saw it, the child would come back from the outside world in a state of stress and the mother would be a regulator of those negative states. Neuroscience now indicates that 'play' experiences, which we know start at the end of the second month, and which is also associated with an intense growth spurt of the brain, are central to development. The attachment to the mother is therefore not only minimising negative states but she's maximising positive states. (Schore and Carroll 2001)

Chapter 3
Preparing for Life Story Therapy

When I first started life story work in SACCS in 1997, I was clearly informed that I was not a therapist, but was a social worker working therapeutically with children. I have often considered this statement, and where the line appears between 'therapy' and 'therapeutic'. The word 'therapy' comes from the Greek '*therapeia*', which in turn translates to 'be attentive to':

> ...wanting to help children whose faith in adults is slim, whose experience of adults is dire and whose cynicism is often entrenched and well founded. Therapists have to communicate in a way that might reach these individuals. (Hunter 2001)

The therapist is therefore an individual who provides therapy and is attentive to the needs of the child. Winnicott (1971) identifies the importance of the 'potential space' that needs to be provided to allow the traumatized child to feel safe, secure and contained by the therapist responsible for the maintenance of the environment. He considered that therapy required the child to be engaged in exploring her past and to relate her internal world with her external world. This approach should encourage children to identify the journey and its consequences for the present. By combining the two, the child is able to explore new avenues from old, and to create new thinking, new meaning and safer connections.

Therapy is a space for the child to externalize her internal world through the use of play, art, narration, stories, movement and/or cognitive engagement. The approach can be non-directive, directive, verbal, nonverbal or a combination of both. The outcome of such engagements is to provide children with the opportunity to recover from their trauma; to understand their part in it and recognize that they no longer need to be held within it. For this to happen, the therapist has a primary task, that being to make a safe relationship, which can demonstratively provide a safe, strong, dependable and contained environment.

The context of the relationship between therapist and client and the potential for the client to heal is often dependent on the ability of the therapist to contain, to be patient, to model understanding and calmness. He must be able to understand transference and countertransference, as well as possessing the skills of interpretation and facilitation (Baldwin 1987; Hardham 1996).

Therapists are registered within their disciplines, and each discipline will have professional ethics and values which underpin it. There are courses which are delivered throughout the world and, once qualified, many therapists work in the independent field and engage with multi-complex children. I am clear that training and continuous professional development is essential to ensure best practice and protection of children. Most courses are of two years' duration, they demand competency as well as theory, and there are professional bodies that maintain the high standards required. Currently there are a multitude of therapy approaches available to traumatized children, and many choose to be non-direct in their nature.

In therapeutic work with children, there have been great strides in creating care teams around the child, these are 'circle teams' and 'teams around the child'. The therapist, to be successful, must work with the team, to report to and be responsive to the aims and outcomes desired.

> If [therapists] are to work effectively with accommodated young people, they have to take their place in the circle of people holding the safety net. (Hunter 2001)

This is also supported in the findings of Wilson (2001), who states that therapy cannot be secretive, because if it remained so, it would underpin the secretive nature of abuse. She argues that therapists need to be heard, but that they must also listen to the team around the child. Such integration will outweigh any confidentiality that is thought to be at risk. It is generally accepted that the most productive therapy is that which is centred round the child and supports the child's best interest.

Therapy, though, has to have direction, a process whereby all those involved understand where they are, where they have been and where they are going. In most therapy interactions, the child is engaged with the intervention and encouraged to explore her internal world. There is a requirement to ask the child questions which promote the relationship, and therefore the therapist needs to be involved and not a passive, watchful assessor.

The therapist has several roles within the engagement, but all therapy has differing processes. Some therapists who work with children as their primary clients regard work with the child as a single, exclusive activity between the therapist and the child; some therapists work with the child with other workers in the room acting as 'mirrors'; some therapists work with both the child and the primary carer in approaches such as Theraplay or life story work; some therapists work with groups of children, and others with children and their families. Whatever the approach, the role of the therapist is the same: to witness the child's story; to hold the child at the centre of the interaction; and to advocate for the child's best interest.

The therapist is crucial to the child's recovery, but as a member of the support network around the child, he is also responsible to the other members of the team. The 'team around the child' consists of significant adults who are able to work together to support the child and the family. In some of the states in Australia, the same is true of the 'circle programme', which is based on providing foster carers with a support structure of professionals who can guide the care task and provide resources to the placement to promote its success. Systems that promote the concepts of 'team around the child' hold that communication among all of the adults, the carer and the child is crucial, and so the therapist must share information, themes and concerns with the team as a whole.

More recently, I have begun to take the sessions at the home of the child, wherever this may be. I am certain that this has added value to the relationship, whereby the child feels in control of the environment, and is able to see me leave, rather than the other way round. I have also found that the time of the therapy is equally important. Children do not want to be taken out of school to attend what might be a very difficult session, only to have to return and try to cope internally with the information exchanged, and externally with school demands. For this reason, I only see children after school hours and in view of the office hours of most 'rentable' places on offer, home is often the only option.

Wherever the therapy takes place, the important thing for the child is that the therapist is a capable and strong person who can convey clear messages to the child, which are:

- I will protect you.
- I care about you.
- I will not let you hurt yourself or me.
- I am not overwhelmed by your experience or your feelings.

- I know it is not your fault.
- I know we can face these issues together.
- I know you are going to be OK.
- I will help you be OK.

The therapist can then clarify to the child why it is important to consider the past and examine those events slowly, thoughtfully and, above all, together. Rather than informing the child about the events and consequences of the same, the therapist needs to listen to and value the child's perceptions, her own ideas and her current feelings, and to clarify the link between these and the behaviours that she has adopted as a result. It is only then that the therapist can assist the child to accept reality, to understand her own power and set aside the burden of the past in favour of the opportunities of her future.

The therapy space

Wherever life story therapy takes place, the environment has to represent safety and containment to all those involved. As with all therapy, the environment must lend itself to the purpose of the exercise. Life story therapy has, amongst its objectives, that of working on attachment between the child and the primary carer. It is clear that the more stable, the more available and the more familiar the environment, the more likely it is that the relationship can be progressed. The ideal that the therapy space should be a stage for the child to express her feelings and to encourage her thinking is real; I would add that there is an equal need for the primary carer to share the same billing.

Preparation for life story therapy intervention

The following strategies have proved extremely useful in the preparation process for intervention.

In 2004 I created a simple model called HIDE (an acronym for the four principles detailed below) to help members of the SACCS recovery team to ensure that the children that they worked with were not able to hide from them. All too often we allow the neediest children to manipulate their way to the back of the group they occupy, so as not to be seen. The model insists that the therapist consider four key areas:

1. **History:** To ensure that there is a clear understanding of the child's past and that this is robust. The therapist needs to have an understanding of the child's family history and significant factors that have led to the child being referred. When the child knows that the therapist is familiar with the story she represents, she is able to engage with this in mind.

2. **Inner working model:** The therapist needs to have considered the child's early life experience and to have formed a hypothesis about how the child views herself, the adults who have care of her (and authority over her) and the world as a place to belong. This 'internal working model' can change, and therapy should contribute to the process whereby the child achieves a more positive internal working model.

3. **Development:** Many children who are presented to me as needing life story therapy do not merit the labels that are pinned on them. I am not saying that ADHD (for example) is not a significant issue for many children, but in my experience, many children who show signs of such a diagnosis learn to engage and to develop as we work with them; as their preoccupation with trauma is reduced, they have more capacity to recover. The same can be said for other learning difficulties. The need for clear understanding of the child's development, including physical, emotional, spiritual and cognitive aspects, is paramount to engagement in the recovery process with the child.

4. **Environment:** Some of our children come from the most awful neglect situations:

> The house was dark and cold; both girls were in the corner of the room. Clare was playing with a plastic bag and Penny was knocking her head against a wall. Penny hid her face and did not speak. All her visible skin and clothes were very dirty. Her hair was matted, and she had shadows under her eyes. Georgie called her but she did not respond. Georgie sat smoking, flicking ash into an overflowing bag of rubbish. (Rose and Philpot 2005)

Children become accustomed to their environment and their own response to it; this becomes their normality and they experience a kind of safety in it. We identify these children and the risks that they face and remove them to environments that are more healthy, safe, organized and appropriate for the best interests of the child:

> ...the house was warm, with a lot of space for the children to play. The carers have ensured that each child has their own bedroom and a play room on the ground floor. There are plentiful toys and stimulation for the children will be encouraged through the array of education based play. (Rose and Philpot 2005)

However, because this is not normal for the child, on entry to this environment she may become distressed; it represents a hostile world for her and presents the challenges of new learning, trepidation and fear of what might happen and when if she 'breaks' this new place. This often leads to a child trying to recreate the chaos that is normal for her, and we struggle with this, as we cannot sense the enormous stress we place on our children.

The child's placement: Holding children at the CENTRE of all we do

I have come up with a simple acronym – CENTRE – which can be used when considering whether a child's home is good enough. The placement must have a clear 'Culture', understandable by all who interact within and without it. The 'Environment' must be supportive of the task; it must be clean, welcoming, consistent, owned, stable and warm. The placement must have the ability to 'Nurture' the child, to provide reliable, dependable and committed adults to role-model best care and to demonstrate love and warmth to the child. The therapeutic care 'Team' (be that in a residential or a family setting) must be supportive, educated and inclusive; it is vital that the members think together, act as one and support the team through clear and appropriate communication. 'Relationships' within the placement need to model, commentate on and work through processes of attachment, engagement and maintenance. Finally, 'Education' of the team as well as the children within the placement is essential, both formally and informally, as EU care regulations continue to change alongside developments in pedagogy.

Good care and safe environment

Every child has a right to be happy, healthy, safe and successful. It is the responsibility of us all to work with children and their families and to help keep them together whenever possible. When this is not achievable, it is our duty to ensure that there is an outstanding system of public care. A service which is committed to children and young people, that identifies and champions their best interest. A service that provides well trained and committed carers and with a mind set that demands nothing less than what we would wish for all children. 'Good care' means that a child is provided with a sense of security, safety and containment which will assist her healthy development and essential need to self-regulate. As the child begins to accept that the adults around her can protect, love and care for her, she can be helped to recapture her sense of self.

Children being cared for in substitute care, especially those who have experienced poor care and abuse, may have particular behavioural issues that create challenges for those caring for them. Often these children have been let down, become entrenched in negative outlooks, and are angry and confused about the situation they find themselves in. Children may have sexual difficulties, particularly around their behaviour towards other children and adults, as well as towards themselves. This challenges thinking around the provision of safe environments, where psychodynamic approaches need to be utilized to assist recovery and where children can model attachment with their primary carers. It is important that planning safe care is clearly understood by all those working with traumatized children.

Children who have experienced trauma through exposure to violence, neglect, sexual and/or emotional harm often find themselves living in chaos, a chaos that may exist in their internal as much as their external world. As they have experienced danger and fear, they have become accustomed to that state and feel 'comfortable' with it. Children who have been traumatized, and/or who have received poor care may have developed a damaged self-image whereby they view themselves as uncared for and unlovable. They may see their therapeutic parents as unloving and untrustworthy, and subsequently see all carers in the same light. When such children come into a care environment, the provision of good quality care can come as a shock or a threat, or seem 'abnormal'. In these cases children may attempt to recreate their chaos, and in doing so they may put themselves or others at risk, or terminally upset their therapeutic parents and/or their placement.

> Trauma significantly alters baseline physiological arousal levels in children. Children are likely to benefit from environments of care which pay attention to their mood, focus on adjusting sensory stimulation to promote patterns of effective physiological modulation, and engage predictable strategies. (Mitchell 2008)

I have observed that children who have been subject to trauma are likely to be anxious and hypervigilant; they are often aroused in situations where they expect harm, or expect the trauma to be revisited on them. This state of awareness is exhausting, and can cause the child to be preoccupied with fear and anxiety. Preoccupation with the past and wariness of the present mean that there is less of the child existing. In the present, therefore she is unable to learn quickly, or to cope well in various situations, and is at a disadvantage in comparison to healthy peers within the community. This preoccupation often results in frustration for the therapeutic parents (who may have expectations for the child to behave herself, to learn, to feel safe and loved), because it can lead to the child not being able to think, listen or act in positive way – she remains fixed in her past. When introduced into a more ordered and 'safe' environment, she may interpret it as unsafe, disordered and an environment to be rejected. Not surprisingly, this in itself can affect the opportunity to complete, let alone undertake, crucial tasks, which are essential for children to reach their full potential.

Good care requires therapeutic parents to be available for children to explore and make sense of the things that have happened to them, and the feelings, emotions and behaviours that they communicate. Often there is a lack of information, or explanation, but the opportunity to think with a therapeutic parent supports the child to think out (externalize) her preoccupation and resolve some of her chaos.

Traumatized children require routine, predictability and consistency, rather than excess of material provision, freedom and 'love'. If a therapeutic parent is able to deliver stability within the care environment, the child can become held by the knowledge that events run according to a predictable, reliable routine: meals are available at set times; bedtime routines are clear and contained; therapeutic parents carry out primary care tasks, and rules are adhered to – all this is part of good care. When routines are not maintained, traumatized children can become anxious and revert to the chaos that they are familiar with. When things go wrong and stability is affected, the carer needs to explain the reasons for this and take action which is clear, visible and effective. By taking the time to reassure the child, the therapeutic parent is able to demonstrate a capacity to cope. If the therapeutic parent is able to role-model the ability to cope with the unexpected and communicate the process of coping, this will enable the child to learn from the experience and begin to model the same.

It is important that therapeutic parents and others who provide caring or nurturing environments are clear about their rules and expectations around behaviour. All those providing care for children need to have clear statements of purpose which include a description of the rules, and of the consequences if they are not followed. These rules deliver a sense of safety only if they are 'policed' and enforced. (Many traumatized children will have poor experiences of rules, consistency and discipline.) Clearly, the consequences that are set out should be applicable and achievable – if not, the rule will be challenged, and if it is not robust, the rule itself damages the safety of the placement.

With boundaries come consequences, as already stated, but it is often through these consequences that real learning takes place. When a child does something wrong, the role of the therapeutic parent is to think with the child about the behaviour or actions taken and to consider ways to deal with these. Creating opportunities for children to revisit the boundary and the behaviour demonstrated allows reflection and promotes the idea of change.

Therapeutic parents need to encourage children to show their feelings by acknowledging the child's emotions, both overt and covert. Reflecting thoughts that the therapeutic parent has with the child is a helpful process, i.e. commenting about where feelings are, how they are coped with and exploring where they stem from. Giving a child the opportunity to communicate her feelings by working through her own actions and reactions, as well as those of others, is essential for developing coping skills for the future. Therapeutic parents need to understand themselves, and to be aware of their own feelings, how they communicate, and how they use internal and external controls. This process of 'knowing the self' assists therapeutic parents to identify their feelings and share with the child how they manage difficult situations.

As the child develops, and more and more opportunities are thought through, and as the child begins to make mistakes and 'fall down', the carer needs to provide support, trust and respect in helping the child 'get up again'. The reality of working with children should not be measured in terms of how many times they 'fall down', but of how many times they 'get up'. Experiences of coping, trusting and seeking and receiving support provide crucial learning opportunities which underpin the development of social relationships.

The care of therapeutic parents is also vital to the provision of safe care and safe environments. There is a need to educate therapeutic parents to meet not the minimum requirements of the task, but to fulfil it optimally. There are dangers of uncontained transference and countertransference and these need to be recognized; professional supervision and group consultancy can cater for conscious and unconscious processes, and good senior management can support carers to be professional, caring, informed and healthy.

Finally, all those in a safe caring environment need to know that it is working and providing the opportunities for children to develop into caring adults, and in some cases, successful and nurturing parents. Outcome models of assessments are positive tools which provide evidence of progress, opportunities for development and common frameworks to aid collective thinking and planning. It is important to know where a child is and where we would like the child to be; it is vital that the child can understand this and contribute to the task. For this to happen the outcome model must involve the child and she must have the opportunity to ultimately direct her own future.

Creating a contract for the therapy to take place

I believe that the best way to create contracts with children is by designing them together from scratch. This permits the child to engage in what is right and acceptable, rather than presenting a 'fait accompli'; it also allows discussion about the contract and reasons for certain things to be included and others not, for example:

> Child protection: If we say anything that might cause us to be concerned about the safety or wellbeing of any child, then we will need to tell someone who can make it safe for that child. Richard will make sure that we know what is to be reported and any other things that might have to happen to make us all OK.

Other areas to be included might be the time and frequency of sessions; confidentiality of sessions; who can see the material created; acceptable behaviour; procedure for stopping sessions; and what to do if the child gets upset.

Structure and boundaries are also important to set out. To this end it is a good idea to introduce a 'welcome book' which explains life story to the child, the carer, and all those around the child who have involvement in the process. Rachel Oliver, a life story therapist with SACCS, designed the Welcome Book reproduced below, which I have used extensively in my own work with children in the UK.

My Life Story: Welcome Book

What happens before we start?

Before we begin your Life Story Therapist will talk to people about you and how they have been involved in your life.

Some people may have a different story, but that's OK. Everybody has a different story, different memories and different understandings. Your Life Story Therapist will have the chance to understand what everyone says and to bring it all together so that they can help you to make sense of things.

> **How do we work together?**
>
> We won't start Life Story straight away as we need to get to now each other. To do this we will play some games together and begin to work out what feelings that we have and how we can understand where these come from.
>
> When we start Life Story, we will meet once every two weeks with your main care provider. These meetings will take place on the same day at the same time so that we can all get used to the sessions and feel comfortable in talking about the past.
>
> In Life Story Therapy we will record what we do on wallpaper, each time we meet, we can unroll the paper and remind ourselves with what we have done in past meetings. We will all have a chance to draw, paint and write on the paper, so you will be given art things such as pens, felt tips, glue and paint.

> questions

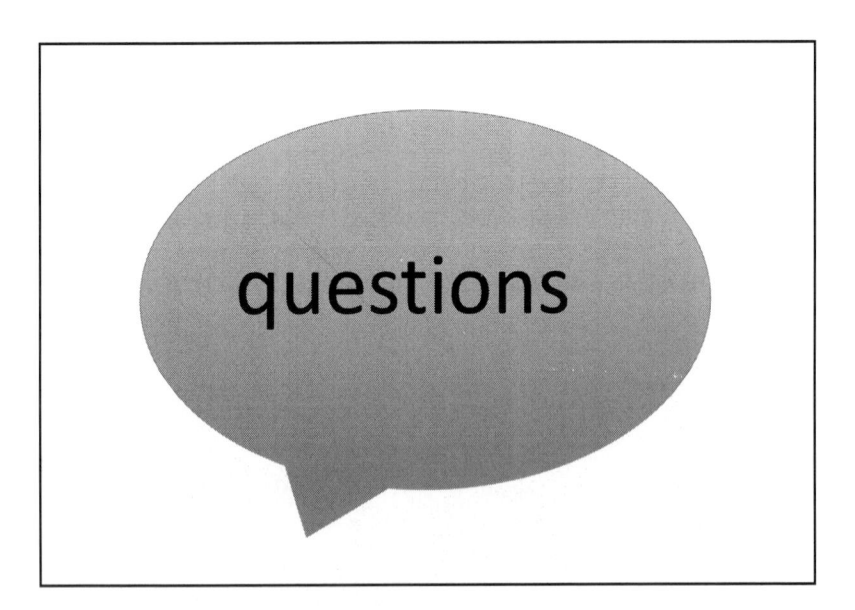

Figure 3.1 The SACCS Welcome Book, designed by Rachel Oliver

It is important that all those involved in the therapy understand the purpose, the aims and the objectives of the service. The Welcome Book and the contract agreement support this; however, the environment is crucial to the success of the therapy intervention.

Therapy requires the art of relationship making, and to this end the quality of relationship in the process of life story therapy is crucial. In the next few chapters I introduce play tasks, each of which aims to promote engagement between the child and the adult. Alongside relationship building is the need to provide safety and security around the child for the sessions, and inevitably this means the introduction of boundaries. The life story therapist must consider and enact clear boundaries around the intervention, which are understood by both the therapist and by the therapeutic parent (primary carer). I find that contracts among all those involved are a good basis for creating an agreed, safe environment for the sessions to take place.

Part II

The Stages of Life Story Therapy

Each course of life story therapy should be unique to the child that you are working with; however, there is a need for structure, and a flow. The following chapters will illustrate a step-by-step process for completing the life story intervention through preparation, information gathering and relationship building. There is a series of useful direct work exercises to assist the internalization stage, and finally recommendations for creating the life story book.

Chapter 4
Stage 1: The Information Bank

> If you really want to understand how a child is functioning in the present, you need to understand their personal history because the brain more than anything is an historical organ. It stores experiences. If you understand the personal experiences of the child, you will understand a lot about how different systems in the brain are organized. So it's very important to take a high quality developmental history of that child. One of the most important factors in a good developmental history is getting some understanding and some insights about the childrearing beliefs and practices of their caregiver, which you can usually get by asking them about their family and the way they were raised. (Perry 2003)

Life story therapy needs excellent sources of information to allow the therapist to understand the HIDE model (see page 63) of each child that he works with. Information comes from the various people and paperwork that reflect the child's life, as well as the life of her parents.

Often I am asked how to access information, about the problems around privacy and confidentiality, and how the information collated is stored.

The following reiterates some of the guidance first featured in *The Child's Own Story* (Rose and Philpot 2005), and incorporates new ideas to assist the reader.

Case study: Jade
Jenny Johannsen was born in 1971 and married David Porter in 1994, having recently given birth to her first child (Deborah). Files suggest a good mainstream schooling experience followed by several jobs and work schemes.

First involvement with Social Services was when Deborah was found in the care of a family friend who was registered as a Schedule one offender. She had been found to be in some distress and later a medical confirmed that she had been sexually hurt by this family friend. David Porter was later found in a comatose state nearby. Deborah was subject to an adoption soon after this event.

Jade's parents had been evicted from a local housing trust and had moved into a squat in a very poor area of the town. The couple were targeted by locals and lived in fear as a result of local people finding out about the abuse of their daughter and the friendship they subsequently continued with the alleged perpetrator. Jenny Johannsen and David Porter divorced in 1998 and Jenny was described as being poorly organized and prone to bouts of depression.

Jenny later met and married Robert Sallis, whom she met at a local day centre. The marriage took place in 2003. Mr Sallis was born in 1966 into a sibling group of 12 (a travelling family who settled in Yorkshire). Mr Sallis had attended a school for children with learning difficulties and was being supported by Social Services to live within the community. He had never held gainful employment. Mr Sallis was also prone to violent temper episodes which often ended with his arrest and placement within hospital settings, subject to various secure placement orders.

During her pregnancy with Jade, Jenny felt that she was unsupported by their families, and Social Services' involvement seemed limited to Adult Services intervention. There was concern about the parents' capacity to meet the needs of the expected child; the midwife referred her concerns to Social Services and it was agreed that Jenny alone would be assessed regarding her parenting skills. The family moved out of the squat to a house in a very large council estate and found themselves immediately targeted by local youths who would taunt them and throw fireworks, bottles and rocks at the home. Robert Sallis was arrested on 12 September, the day before Jade's birth, having attacked two youths with a machete, causing one youth to receive fatal injuries. The attack was a response to these youths pouring petrol through the letterbox of the home.

In August 2003 Jenny had been involved in a car crash and sent to hospital; she had suffered some abdominal pain and remained in hospital for the rest of her pregnancy. Jade was born on 13 September and weighed 7lb 1oz – a healthy child, giving rise to no medical concerns and scoring 9 on the Apgar score.

As soon as Jade was born, there was an application by Social Services for a care order. This was agreed and Jade was placed on an interim care order. The interim care order continued until August 2004 when a supervision order was agreed by all present. Jenny had demonstrated her ability to care for Jade, with the help of her Auntie Gina, who had moved Jenny to her home in the neighbouring town. (Robert had been placed on remand for the death of the teenager he had attacked and awaited court action, but it was felt that he would not be released in the short or medium term.)

Jenny and Gina did not get on well, and Gina told Jenny to leave the home, but successfully persuaded Jenny to leave Jade with her. This situation did not last long; within two months Jade was made subject to respite care arrangements, and over the next year she was placed in the care of 13 different families. Each time she was returned to her great-aunt and on each occasion referred by various professionals as being at risk of emotional harm as a result of her great-aunt's dislike for her.

In March 2007 attempts at rehabilitating Jade with her great-aunt were clearly failing. On the last occasion she had returned to her foster home with bruises on her back and unexplained marks around her mouth. A child protection investigation found that Jade had been hurt by Gina's partner, and it later transpired that he had sexually harmed her. Jade was again placed in a foster home in April 2007.

Jade's brother Richard was born on 30 October 2007. Again medical staff expressed concerns about Jenny's attitude to the baby and her family. Richard was accommodated three days later, and Jenny was referred to the Adult Mental Health Team.

Within four weeks of being placed with her new carer Jade began to disclose sexual events involving family friends of her previous foster carers and of people who stage at her great-aunt Gina's home. Soon after, Richard was moved in to live with Jade and her carers. Concerns were expressed by her carers and by workers observing contact for Jade. Another concern was that Jenny was pregnant again. By April, Jade was refusing to go to contact, becoming very clingy to her foster carer, who also expressed concern at this time about the heightened sexuality demonstrated by Jade towards Richard.

In 2009 Jade was referred for adoption. A full care order and placement order were agreed, and she was placed with a family called Brown. Unfortunately this placement failed. In January 2010 Jade (now aged 6) stated that she wanted to be dead, to be rid of those around her, and free. She began to self-harm and on several occasions was seen to attack the family cat – on one occasion trying to push the cat into an open fire in the main room. In March 2010, following a further stay in respite care, she was referred to a residential placement, and placed in May 2010. Jade was reported as being violent, talking of death and showing 'obsessive' behaviour – although the obsessive part has not been recorded with detail.

All in all, Jade has been in 32 placements. Her schooling has clearly suffered and she has attended six different education centres (partly as a result of moves out of the local authority area). Her school behaviour has caused concern, mainly around her destructive actions and her inability to make friends.

There are many ways in which to approach the information above. As assessment workers, we need to make sense of the story, to understand the patterns and to work on the sequencing that the story provides. Most assessors would look at identifying a family tree; others would be considering a chronology, whilst some might choose a 'life snake'. A life snake is a visual device in the form of a snake: at one end of the snake the child's birth date is placed, and at the other end the current date. Working along the snake, the therapist would place information that pertains to the events that are known to have occurred e.g. moving house, school, care episodes.

Over the years I have tried to work with a more methodical process of information banking, responding to the need to have as much information as possible.

The first thing to do, in order to make sense of Jade's story, is to break it down into 'bite-size chunks'. Many years ago, social workers often used 'movement boxes' to help understand the flow of a case transfer summary. The history flowchart allows each piece of information to be considered separately, and affords the assessor the opportunity to clarify the relationships between the pieces. I have started this process below to help the reader to understand it.

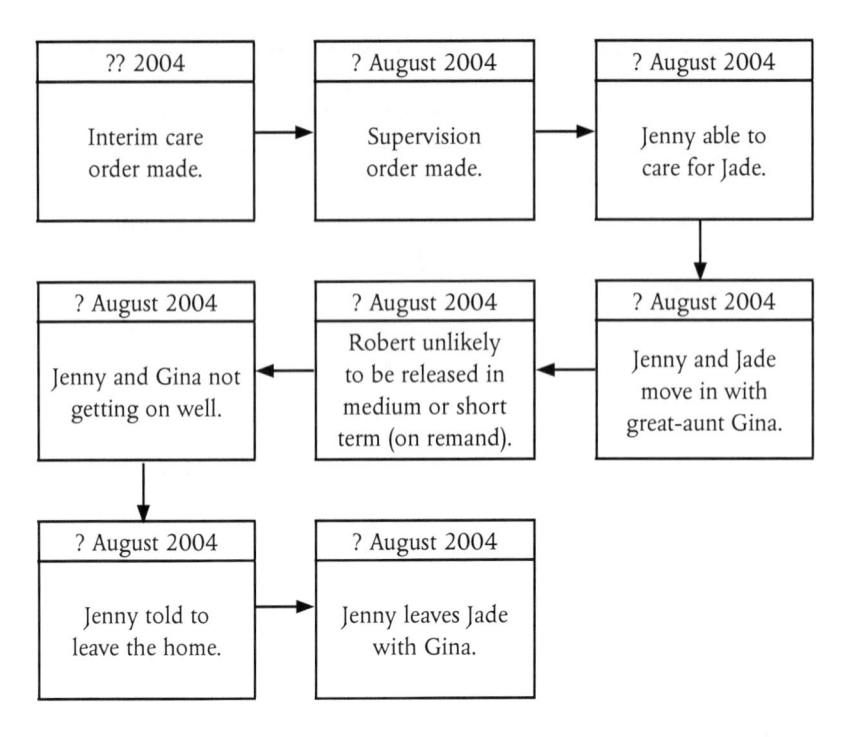

```
┌─────────────────┐    ┌─────────────────┐    ┌─────────────────┐
│    ?? 2004      │    │  ? August 2004  │    │  ? August 2004  │
├─────────────────┤    ├─────────────────┤    ├─────────────────┤
│   Interim care  │───▶│   Supervision   │───▶│   Jenny able to │
│   order made.   │    │   order made.   │    │   care for Jade.│
└─────────────────┘    └─────────────────┘    └─────────────────┘
                                                        │
                                                        ▼
┌─────────────────┐    ┌─────────────────┐    ┌─────────────────┐
│  ? August 2004  │    │  ? August 2004  │    │  ? August 2004  │
├─────────────────┤    │ Robert unlikely │    ├─────────────────┤
│ Jenny and Gina  │    │ to be released  │    │ Jenny and Jade  │
│  not getting    │◀───│ in medium or    │◀───│  move in with   │
│   on well.      │    │ short term      │    │ great-aunt Gina.│
│                 │    │ (on remand).    │    │                 │
└─────────────────┘    └─────────────────┘    └─────────────────┘
         │
         ▼
┌─────────────────┐    ┌─────────────────┐
│  ? August 2004  │    │  ? August 2004  │
├─────────────────┤    ├─────────────────┤
│   Jenny told    │───▶│  Jenny leaves   │
│  to leave the   │    │  Jade with      │
│     home.       │    │     Gina.       │
└─────────────────┘    └─────────────────┘
```

Figure 4.1 Jade's story in movement boxes

Figure 4.1 is a visual representation of the information set out in the case study above (pages 76–9). The life story therapist will need to break down the whole story into movement boxes, and, on average this will probably require 400 to 500 boxes.

Once the boxes have been completed, the next task is to consider each one as a separate entity so that we can begin to examine the information given and the questions it might raise.

```
┌─────────────────┐
│  ? August 2004  │
├─────────────────┤
│ Jenny and Jade  │
│  move in with   │
│ great-aunt Gina.│
└─────────────────┘
```

Taking this box as an example, we need to ask three questions:

1. What do I as the life story therapist need to know?
2. What do I consider might be the things that Jade (now doing life story) would ask or like to know?

3. And, crucially, what may not be safe to share?

It is best to free-think questions under each of the main domains, and for the box above, the assessor will compile the following:

1. What do I need to know?
- Who is great-aunt Gina?
- Where is the home?
- What was the historical relationship like between the main characters?
- Why is great-aunt Gina involved now?
- How did Jenny feel about the move?

2. What might Jade ask?
- Did she like me?
- Did she like my mum?
- What was the home like?
- Did Dad come too?
- Are there any pictures of her?

3. What might not be safe to share?
- the past relationships
- great-aunt Gina's personal history
- the issues between Jenny and her extended family.

As we begin to assemble the questions for each box, it becomes clearer that the task of the life story is not simply to retell the story of the child from the recording of one or two voices. I have found inestimable value in life story work, as lost opportunities are rediscovered, and often, stories full of inaccurate facts have been integrated by the child as her history.

Once the boxes are complete, it will often be the case that the assessor has identified hundreds of questions for himself and hundreds of possible questions from the child. These questions need to be considered and addressed to the possible information holders. To this end, identifying information banks is the next step. With the story of Jade, identifying the people and the paperwork is the next task. This is best achieved by using a simple 'ecomap' approach and I have reproduced the ones from the 2004 book (Rose and Philpot 2004) as useful examples (see Figure 4.2).

82　Life Story Therapy with Traumatized Children

a) Information gathering

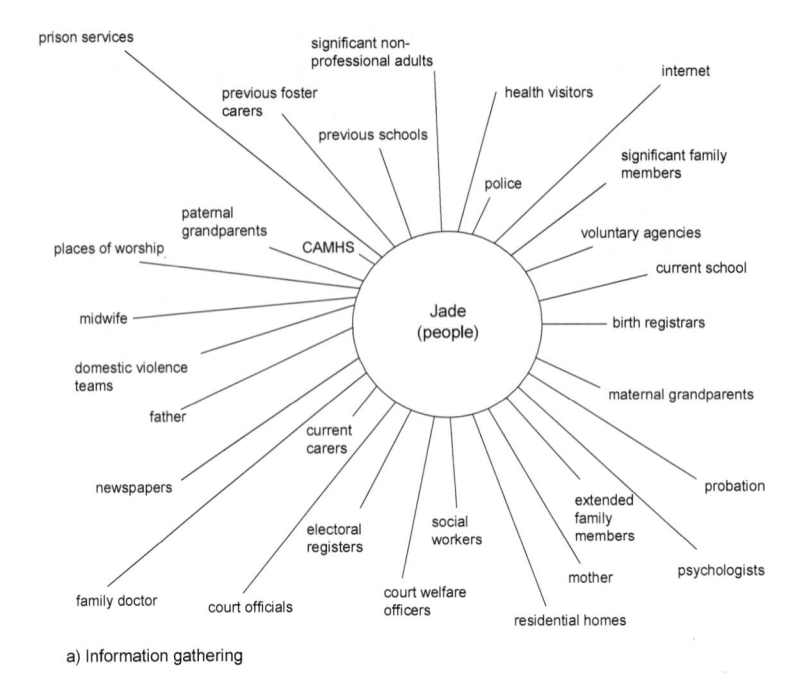

Figure 4.2 Jade's story: ecomaps

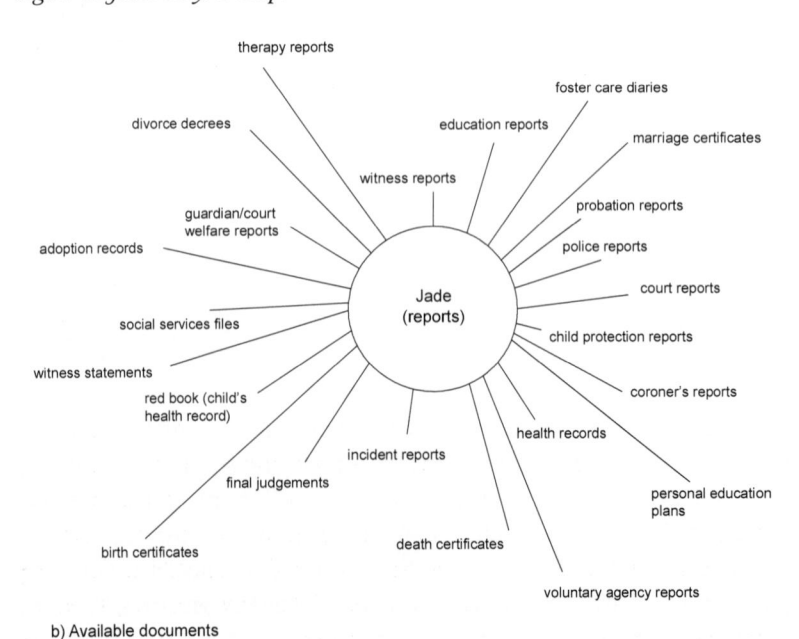

b) Available documents

Figure 4.2 Jade's story: ecomaps cont.

Once the ecomaps have been completed, the assessor then sorts all the questions from the three lists he has compiled, placing them in chronological order below the name of the appropriate individual, or the relevant source of documentation. There will quickly be an identified visual representation of those who have most information to give and those that have least.

The reality, of course, is that you must have a clear understanding of what information you have, what information you need and where the information is located. For individuals you cannot see, you can write to them and enclose a list of questions that you feel are of most use to you. In my experience, the more specific you can be in requests for information, the more comfortable the informer is likely to be. For those you decide to see, there is a readymade list of questions to work through, which, again, will structure the interview and give focus to the information required.

As for written information and access to records, this too is identified through the ecomap exercise, and the writer simply needs to order the information from the various holders when it comes to documents such as birth, death, marriage and divorce papers. For access to social work files, medical records and police reports, the assessor needs to consider the permission gates that need to be opened. As an example: when it comes to medical records, these may be made available by permission of the patient or their representative/corporate parent. A simple letter giving authority for access may apply.

Birth certificates are public records and available for a fee. I have never had trouble accessing birth certificates for the children I work with, and most times this is achieved over the telephone or online. Birth certificates are essential to locate, as they hold so much of the history of the child and the link to their heritage. In the past I have located certificates for three generations of a child and through that accessed their brothers, sisters and uncles and aunts. We can achieve so much for children by spending this time collating their 'broken shards' and making sense of who they are.

Over the last 15 years I have found ways to access all the information that I can possibly identify as being useful and ultimately in the best interests of the children I work with. This is not to say that confidentiality and privacy has been trounced, but by thoughtful, persuasive and sometimes imaginative approaches, the information is brought to life.

Assessing information is an art form in itself; in *The Child's Own Story* (Rose and Philpot 2005) I detailed a clear interview process for readers to understand the importance of interview skills and the manner of engagement between interviewer and interviewee.

Techniques for interviewers
The rapport stage
This is the stage when we aim to reassure those whom we want to interview, to allay any fears or misapprehensions they may have and help them to feel at ease in our company and with our questions.

At this stage we will wish to gauge the person to whom we are talking, to try to assess their skills and intellectual capacity. How do they deal with someone they have never met before? Are they innately suspicious? Do they simply seek reassurance? What we want to do is to communicate to them that we are interested in them and that what they have to say is important to us, which in itself is a way of assuring them that they are important and that we value them.

The first rule at this stage, on meeting the interviewee, is to talk about everything but the subject to hand! Give them the chance to talk about themselves. We might discuss our journey, the weather, where we are meeting them. (If it is in their own home this will afford ample opportunity for them to tell us about themselves.) At this time, too, we need to take account of the environment. Is the television left on? Is there loud music? Are there other adults about? Are there children around? Very often photographs of family members, children long since removed from the interviewee's care or deceased grandparents, will afford the person the opportunity to discuss and reminisce about those things important to them. One woman visited for a life story interview had very obviously spent a lot of time collecting and collating photographs, because she had a pile of them available when the interviewer arrived. This was her way of entering into the discussion and prompting what she could remember.

Whatever is said to us, no matter how trivial it is or how unrelated it is to the reason why we are actually there, the interviewer should show that he is interested and that he is listening, and not just coming into the person's life for the interview, carrying it out and moving on, as if it were some mechanical process.

Rapport can also be about language. How articulate is the person? Is English their first language? If it is not, would they feel more comfortable, when it comes to the actual interview, to have an interpreter present?

It is important to know if the interviewee has a hearing problem. I once went to see an older married couple, and the man was very quick to assume all kinds of things about the visit, about which he needed reassuring. The conversation continued and then the man said that he needed to correct his wife's hearing aid, which was not working. Had he not received the reassurance he needed, he would not have done that, and what she had to say would never have been heard.

The most important impression to be relayed is that the interviewee is a person, and interested in what they have to say. We are not there to judge them but only to listen and record. The simple fact of being listened to may encourage many family members, especially parents, to speak about their accountability, their hopes and their fears. This may be the first time that they have been able to do so as, for various reasons, the court process does not allow it (it is adversarial; the person will be led through his or her evidence; and they may also be advised that some statements will be prejudicial to their case).

The contract stage

This follows the rapport stage and is where, having established with the person why we are there, we agree the parameters of the interview. We make sure that both interviewer and interviewee understand them. There are approaches to take and not to take. For example, a question like: 'How long have I got?' may elicit the answer: 'An hour.' But if the question is: 'What's your timetable for today?' that may well provoke the response: 'I've nothing much on – I can talk to you for as long as you like.'

At the contract stage, too, the interviewer should explain what he means by confidentiality, that is, what he is told will be confidential, except that the interviewer has a duty to report anything that affects the safety of the child. If information is given which would be useful to a third party, then that will be discussed with the interviewee. If anything is to be said which the interviewee would prefer was not to be shared with the child, then that, too, is something which will be discussed.

The interviewer should also make it clear that the person can choose to keep whatever they wish to themselves, and also that they can stop the interview if they want. But it is also important that the person being interviewed knows that any information will be used professionally, sensibly and sensitively. This means ensuring that a parent knows that painful information they give the worker will be imparted appropriately to the child. For example, parents may disclose (possibly for the first time) that they were themselves abused as children, and say that they do not want their child to know that. What this usually means is that they do not want the information to be put to the child as brutally as they have imparted it. The worker should explain that he will say to the child something like: 'Your mummy was hurt in a sex way and that's the cause of her muddles;' or 'Your mummy's daddy could not keep her safe when she was little.' Rape can be expressed as 'Mum had sex when she didn't want to have sex.' Few children are surprised at this information.

On the other hand, people who have abused and may themselves have been abused may well deny any responsibility (even when criminally convicted), and may blame everyone but themselves (even the child), and be manipulative. They may claim that they told the social services department about the child's sexualized behaviour, or that what had happened had occurred at the nursery school and not at home. They may attempt to justify physical abuse on the basis of the child's own allegedly disruptive behaviour. There are ways of confronting abusers with the truth – for example, by quoting other statements or medical reports. If a parent denies it, it is their story, even if it is not what was understood as true. However, if they persist, then their story, along with other (conflicting) accounts, can be presented to the child. Children may get angry at their parents' accounts about what happened to them, and this can be a trigger for the child to give more information and for exploring what else they remember. It may well be, for example, that the child will show that the mother was more involved than social services realized.

Another part of the contract stage concerns how the interview will be recorded. It is better not to use a tape recorder. This can be intimidating to the interviewee; it can distract the interviewer, who may be concerned about whether it is working OK; and if the tape breaks or the machine breaks down, then everything will be lost. It is also the case that life story work takes time, and the time that is required to transcribe an interview of perhaps two or three hours, when a verbatim interview is not required, is not time well spent. An hour-long interview, typically, can be transcribed into 6000 words.

It is much better to take notes, but it should be established, first of all, whether note-taking is acceptable to the person being interviewed. If there are two people meeting the interviewee, then it is best to decide before the meeting who is to take notes.

The interviewee should also be offered a copy of the notes of the meeting. If they cannot read, or cannot read English, then they should have the chance to name someone – a family friend, a solicitor, an interpreter – to whom the notes can be sent. Making the notes available also makes the interviewer accountable.

The interviewer should also explain that he cannot give detailed information about the child – where the child is living or who cares for her – but that information can be given about how she is.

When the contract has been established, the interviewer should seek to confirm that what has been agreed is acceptable, and ask if there is anything more that the interviewee wants to say at this stage.

Free narrative

This is the technique by which the interviewee encourages the person being interviewed to say what they want without being circumscribed by detailed questions.

Interviewers should not arrive with a set of questions to which they are determined to have the answers by the time they leave. This restricts what may be revealed – the unexpected, the unknown – but the engagement rests on a power imbalance that can lead to essential information not being revealed. A conversational interview is likely to reveal more, as well as diminishing the inequality of the encounter. Using set questions also means that the interviewer can be distracted by his determination to proceed from one question to the next until he reaches the last one. This will lead him not to listen as well as he should, not to pick up what is being said, and to go down routes where his own questions take him, rather than directions where answers from the interviewee may lead. Interviewers should always bear in mind the word 'What?' It is with 'What?' that they should begin each question, because it is an information-seeking word. After this, the 'why?' 'where?', 'when?', 'who?' and 'how?' questions can be used to elaborate on the answers.

When considering the first words of a question regarding an event or an incident, it is useful to identify the insinuated meaning behind each one: 'what?' asks for details; 'where?' asks for location; 'when?' asks for the time frame; 'who?' asks for the identity of the people present; and 'how?' asks for the mechanics of the event or incident. 'Why?' is perhaps the most ill-chosen beginning of any question in these interviews because it demands justification, often personal, and carries a suggestion of blame. In sensitive interviews 'why?' is to be avoided in order to ensure that the interview is conducted in a non-judgemental manner. In many situations, the 'why?' can be replaced with 'what?' – for example, 'Why did you do that?' could be rephrased as 'What reasons do you feel there are for the actions taken?'

Thus, questions have to be as open as possible. It is very easy to assume that what *we* have in mind, what *we* want to find out, is all that the person can usefully tell us. This is not so. It is also the case that someone who is wary of saying too much may welcome detailed questions. They know what they are reluctant to say; the interviewer doesn't, and so it is very easy to answer the questions asked and not tell what one is not questioned about.

A very open question can be: 'What do you want to tell me?' The answer may take two minutes or two hours – the listening skills required to deal with the response to such a question are immense, and even note-taking can be a distraction. (The experienced interviewer may very well develop an ability to recall the critical parts of answers without taking notes.)

Listening is a skill, because how many people hear but do not listen?! Listening is about calculated silences; it is about eye contact, body language and posture. It is about the fruitful offering of a 'yes', a nod or some other gesture every now and again. These assure the interviewee of our continuing interest without distracting them or interrupting what they have to say. (It should be noted that silences, eye contact and body language and the way words are used are as useful to the interviewee in understanding the interviewer as vice versa.)

While the aim is to let the person talk, there is also a skill in being aware when to stop them, in case they are going around in circles or repeating themselves. Sometimes a detailed question will have to be asked, in order to get the person back on track.

When the possibilities of free narrative have been exhausted, open questions will cease.

Confirmation

This stage is the summary of the salient points which the interviewee has made in response to the initial question, even if there were then supplementary ones.

Rainbow questions

These are so called because, just as the colours of the rainbow blend into each other at the edges, so the answer to one question can lead to another being asked – and there may be a pot of gold at the end!

This is where we look at historical issues, to elicit information that may need some kind of prompt by a mental association of the person interviewed. They need to be asked what they saw or how they felt, or what they sensed in certain situations. We need this in some detail because first impressions are very important, and in life story work it is critical to know how an adult responded to a child – positively and negatively – and to attempt to offer the child some knowledge of what *did* happen at a certain time as distinct from what he or she *thinks* happened. We may be able to relay to the child some detail, like a smell or a sight, which may have significance for them, dredging up a memory that places them back in time.

For example, if a foster carer is asked what a child was like when she came into the house, the carer may say that the child was crying and bedraggled and carrying two bin liners containing her possessions. But if it is found out that, say, it was raining, or in the middle of the night, that the radio was on, or that music was playing loudly upstairs, or that the smell of the evening meal was wafting into the hallway, these will be much better triggers or scene setters for a child who is wanting to go back and find out about their past. It is details like these that can cause memories to come flooding back.

In such cases a foster carer, for example, could be asked to close her eyes and place herself back in the time when the child arrived. She would then be asked to take the interviewer, step-by-step, from the time of arrival to the child's bedtime. Once this is done, the interviewer could reflect with her on a particular part of that period, such as mealtime or reading a bedtime story that day. This allows the interviewer to have a clearer view of what the child was like – for example, was she used to having a story read to her? Had she cleaned her teeth herself before?

Just as people will sometimes exaggerate, so they will telescope their memories to very basic facts, in order to minimize what has happened or shift the blame onto someone else. It is the rainbow questions that allow the fuller picture to emerge.

However, while we have referred to the process in stages, this should not be dogmatically adhered to – it may be useful sometimes to go from rainbow questions back to the free narrative.

Closed questions

These are related to confirmation. Here the interviewee is asked very specifically if a statement which he or she made was correct. ('You told me this – is it correct?') This is not about the truth or doubting their word, but to confirm their view of what happened, and that should be made plain. It may not have happened, but that does not mean that the person is lying; they simply believe that something occurred in a certain way. However, if the person says that what has been said to them is incorrect, they should not be challenged by saying something like: 'But you told me that…' They should be asked what did happen. They can then set *their* record straight without being accused of fabricating a story.

The summary

This is where a summary of the person's experience of, and with, the child, from all that they have said, is presented to them.

The Colombo question

This is linked to the summary and is named after the television detective who always appeared to have finished questioning his suspects and then, as he was leaving, would put his finger to his brow and say: 'Just one more question.' This is the counterpart of what social workers call 'the door handle question', the question that the person interviewed often asks just as the interviewer has his hand on the door handle ready to leave. These can range from 'Can I see my child?' to 'I haven't told you about…' or 'You haven't asked me about…'

The Colombo question is a double-edged one and can be something like: 'Lots of children talk about the best and the worst times in their lives. Can you think back – what were yours?' Or: 'Can I ask this? You have mentioned your social worker on a number of occasions but what do you really think of her?' Or: 'Would it be OK for me to meet your current partner [or previous partner, if relevant]?'

These questions are asked at this point because they were *not* relevant in the context of earlier questions, and were certainly too detailed to provoke the free narrative. However, they are relevant in the context of what has been said. Sometimes such questions can be asked quite casually, as if prompted by pictures or objects in the room.

The summary and the Colombo questions may seem to bring everything to a close. However, what we have described is a thought-out process and so it must have an ending.

The ending
There is no need now to go back over what has been said: now the intention is to ensure that what has happened has been acceptable and that the interviewee is OK. If they are suffering any distress, then it is necessary to make sure that they have someone to whom they can turn. This could be a friend nearby or – where some past assault has been disclosed – they could be advised that there are places of support such as rape crisis centres, the family doctor or a survivors' group.

The interviewer should finish by thanking the person for seeing him and for the information given. The interviewer should repeat that he has not been there to judge, and will not do so as a result of anything which has been said.

Finding people
Often life story therapy requires the therapist to contact people who were involved with the child many years ago, and sometimes locating these individuals can be complicated and seem an impossible task. In my experience it has always been a positive move to persevere with the detecting of information points.

Case study: Helen
Helen was a child placed in the care of her local authority at nine years of age. Her father was in prison and her mother in a brain injury ward as a result of the violence visited on her by her husband. After a few years in care, it was decided that Helen needed to be placed within a therapeutic residential unit, and it was here that I was asked to provide life story intervention. I identified the material held within the case files and mapped out the movement boxes to enable me to have a clearer understanding of the history of Helen and of her family. Although it was thought that she was an only child, there were hints in the file that there might have been extended family in Ireland.

Some names repeated in the early files suggested that there might have been an older sibling, but also that an aunt was living in the northwest of England. There was an address, but this was more than eight years old. I decided to try and contact the aunt, and looked up the electoral roll registers from the year in question. (Electoral rolls are lists of registered electors with their current address details.) This

> confirmed her full name, which I then entered in a search engine on the internet. There were several people of that name in the same geographical area, but as I had the name of her partner at the time, his name also was searched, and confirmed the address for the current year and that both were still together. I wrote to the aunt and introduced myself and the reason why I wanted to meet with her, and this led to a discussion about Helen's wider family. The long and short of this was that Helen had two older siblings, one a year older and the other two years older, living in Ireland.
>
> I contacted the Health Board in one of the counties in Ireland and arranged to meet with the extended family. This led to arrangements for Helen to meet with her siblings for the first time. She subsequently enjoyed contact three times a year with her family over the next five years of her childhood. The benefits for her were immense at the time and provided her with family connections and a sense of self. Without the detection, she might never have known about her sister and brother, her aunts and uncles, and so would have believed that she was alone in the world.

There are people-finding network sites including Facebook, Twitter, LinkedIn and Friends Reunited; by far the most useful to the life story therapist is the 192.com 'Peoples, Businesses and Places' directory in the UK, or its equivalent in other countries or states. This site allows the seeker to identify where people are by putting a name into the search engine, together with a geographical location. If there is name recognition, all those with that name are identified, and further searches will allow the seeker to identify all those who live with the person, and their address details. It will also identify telephone details, map directions, a picture of the home via Google and other leads to follow.

It has proved very useful to me, but many people I speak to are uncomfortable that all this information, as well as birth certificates and access to confidential files, may be too easy to obtain.

They are justified in thinking this; nevertheless, I have been able to use such information for the best interests of the child I am working with. I would, and have, recommended that people should contact such websites and request that their name and the identity of family members be removed if they feel that privacy is essential for them.

In the USA there is a useful website, www.findagrave.com, which allows researchers and family members to discover where famous people and/or family members have been buried or cremated. It provides a logical pathway to access death records, certificates and coroners' reports; all these sites are driven by the widespread interest in ancestry and genealogy.

It is a sad fact that many of the children that I have worked with have death around them; whether this be a child death through accident or incident, or the death of a family member or significant carer through accident or incident, or deliberate. We are all certain of two things in life: we are born and we die. Children are aware of birth and death. It is the journey between the two that provides the uncertainty. It is for this reason that obtaining death certificates, coroners' reports and newspaper coverage allows the child to talk about and to explore a death, its occurrence and consequences, so as to rule out fantasy, magical thinking and horror and replace these with clarity, evidence and finality.

Case study: Melissa

I once worked with a child who believed that she had killed her younger sister. Her memory was that her mother was cross with her when she found her sister dead. She had sent the child to bed and there was no clarity for her about why she was sent away. The message, which had not been altered, was that the child had been naughty; she had been sent to bed, and the only connection she could make was that she must have done something bad. The only thing that she could recall that was bad was the death of her sister, and so she reasoned that she must have done this deed, as she had been punished.

This child carried this guilt for six years, but within the life story session she was able to take the risk. She actually whispered to me, 'You know I killed (name) don't you?' In this case, I knew of the death and the circumstances surrounding it. We were able to talk about the situation, and I shared the report and the death certificate. I was also able to share with the child her mother's story, the fact that she was not involved in the death, and that her mother did not blame her for it.

Life story therapists need to store information safely, and I recommend using a life story box to accommodate artefacts from the past collected as a result of information gathering. By the end of the process the box should ideally contain photographs, shoes (baby/infant), the red book (development milestone records), birth certificates, celebration cards and religious documents, if applicable. The box should also contain the information files, the movement box charts and session planning. This box is the resource box for the life story work and should be updated as the work continues.

Other uses of the assessment/information bank

The movement boxes process is not confined to life story, and social workers can use the same process when working with problem-solving issues, or thinking cycles of troubled children, and by way of explaining complex care decisions to children. This can be illustrated by the following example (see Figure 4.3):

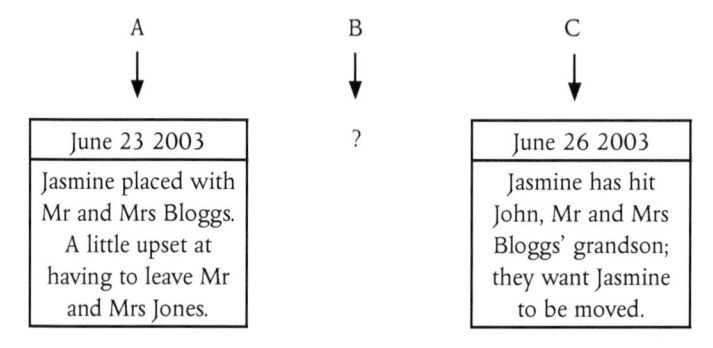

```
       A                    B                    C
       ↓                    ↓                    ↓
┌─────────────┐                          ┌─────────────┐
│ June 23 2003│           ?              │ June 26 2003│
├─────────────┤                          ├─────────────┤
│Jasmine placed with│                    │Jasmine has hit│
│Mr and Mrs Bloggs. │                    │John, Mr and Mrs│
│A little upset at  │                    │Bloggs' grandson;│
│having to leave Mr │                    │they want Jasmine│
│and Mrs Jones.     │                    │to be moved.    │
└─────────────┘                          └─────────────┘
```

Figure 4.3 Using movement boxes to help clarify understanding: Step 1.

When Jasmine was five she was accommodated by the local authority, and stayed in a foster home for almost a year. She displayed a series of concerning behaviours, mostly around sex and pseudo-mature behaviour. Towards the end of the placement she was joined by a three-year-old boy. Her foster family had to move away from the area (some 150 miles), but Jasmine was not allowed to move with them and was placed with a new foster family. Thirteen placements over a period of eight weeks confirmed Jasmine's belief that she was responsible for the breakdown of the first placement. Also, the termination of each placement further confirmed her hypothesis that adults were unsafe and untrustworthy.

The first box, labelled A and the second, labelled C, represent the known facts or events that Jasmine has experienced. Jasmine will try to make sense of such events; she will know of A and C, but may not understand how one led to the other. This gap, we refer to as B. This is the area where distortion and magical thinking can take place. It is this area that we need to explore with Jasmine.

It is important to consider how best to understand the events in B. To do this, we encourage the life story worker to break down potential questions into three areas:

1. What do I (life story worker) need to know?
2. What do I consider the child may want to ask/know?
3. What may be the difficulties that need addressing?

Under each question, bullet-list questions and statements to assist in the thinking process. Here are a few examples:

1. **What do I need to know?**

- When was Jasmine placed?
- Who else was living at Mr and Mrs Bloggs'?
- Why did she leave Mr and Mrs Jones?
- How does Jasmine communicate her distress?

2. **What do I consider the child may want to ask/know?**

- Didn't Mr and Mrs Jones like me?
- Was it because I was really naughty?
- Why did they make me go and stay with Mr and Mrs Bloggs?
- Why did they want to look after me?

3. **What may be the difficulties that need addressing?**

- Jasmine's attachment model.
- History of placement with carers other than Mr and Mrs Jones.
- Consider the views of both Mr and Mrs Jones regarding Jasmine's placement.
- What were the messages given to all three regarding the aims and objectives of the placement when first made?

Traumatized children often will conclude that events happen because of their own role in a situation. Inferred logic operates on the basis that we, as children are brought up with clear messages that adults are always right, therefore, if something is going wrong – it must be our fault. Exploring B enables the child to work through her thinking, feelings and emotions and lets the life story worker engage with this thinking and assist the child to consider and, if appropriate, adopt a more accurate understanding of events.

The next task is to consider Box C and how it relates to the sequence of events. It is helpful to re-letter Box C as Box A, and the following movement box is the new Box C.

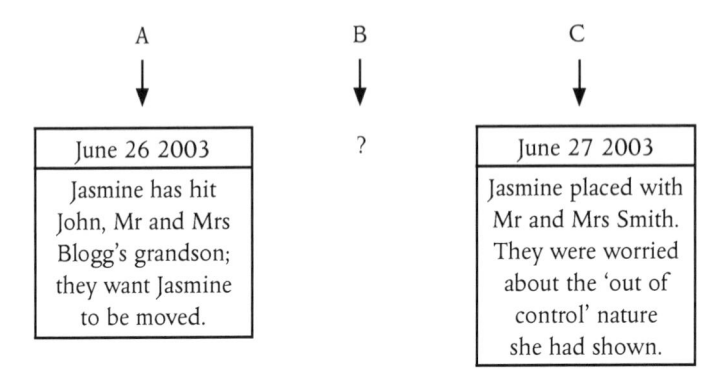

A	B	C
↓	↓	↓
June 26 2003	?	June 27 2003
Jasmine has hit John, Mr and Mrs Blogg's grandson; they want Jasmine to be moved.		Jasmine placed with Mr and Mrs Smith. They were worried about the 'out of control' nature she had shown.

Figure 4.4 Using movement boxes to help clarify understanding: Step 2.

In Jasmine's situation, once all the relevant boxes had been worked through, I was able to identify areas that required information and exploration. That done, I was able to create a clear understanding of the child's placement journey, and then worked with Mr and Mrs Smith to encourage them to think about Jasmine's past.

This process was carried out; I sat with them, thinking about their role as carers, about Jasmine's thinking and feeling processes, and the effects on her of the decisions made for her. Jasmine and her current carers, Mr and Mrs Turner, had concluded that the first family had rejected her and replaced her with a better child, a child that had everything. Jasmine had considered herself to be bad, unlovable and misplaced. Through exploring the stories of various others involved, she was able to consider whether this conclusion was appropriate. Mr and Mrs Turner, the current carers, were able to accept some of the thinking behind the behaviour Jasmine had displayed, and concluded that she had done what she had because of her struggle to make sense of her world.

Over the next year we worked very closely with Jasmine, and together extended the immediate work of saving the placement to the process of life story therapy. During the information gathering process I met with Mr and Mrs Smith, and they agreed to meet with Jasmine when I felt it would be appropriate. Towards the end of the process, I arranged for her to meet her previous carers, Mr and Mrs Jones. Jasmine went through her life story book with them, and they were able to discuss their role, and even brought out keepsakes and photographs of Jasmine which they had kept safe. Jasmine was able to discuss own her past confidently, and was very positive about her future.

Chapter 5

Stage 2: Direct Work with Children

Once the information bank is concluded, and certainly once the process of movement boxing has been achieved, it is time to start building relationships with the child and the primary carer involved. As can be seen in the Welcome Book discussed in Chapter 4, I see children for one hour once each fortnight, on the same day, after school, at the child's home (or placement).

Assessing carers and their capacity to engage in life story therapy

The life story therapy is most successful when it involves the carer in the process. In order to protect the child and the intervention, it is necessary to assess the carer's ability to play a positive and nurturing role. In *The Child's Own Story* I introduced a tripartite approach to life story and put forward the view that the work is an essential part of the attachment process. Since then (and we are now six years further down the life story journey), I am convinced that involving the primary carer in the exploration of their child's journey, where he can hear at first hand the perceptions and misperceptions of the child, provides a unique opportunity for both carer and child to attune.

In recent years, I have witnessed life story work lead to a shared language; a shared experience; emotional congruence and an understanding far beyond that of any other activity. Sadly, I have also witnessed (mainly in the early years of service) cases when this did not happen. Carers were not able to contain the story; emotional angst overwhelmed their coping mechanisms and they were no longer able to engage with the child at a level that was nurturing, containing and supportive. Instead, thoughts unresolved for the carer caused disruption and harm to the placement. I remember one case where I undertook life story therapy, and as soon as I left the home, the child would have an outburst which was directed at the carer, who had been present at the session. It was much later that I found that, within a very short time after I left the session, the carer informed the child of her view of the session and what might come out the next time. Unsurprisingly, the child could not cope with these messages, and her reaction was to sabotage the intervention.

I therefore undertake an assessment of the carer to identify what may be necessary to support him, what is negotiable and, even more important, what is essential. This assessment occurs in the first three months of information gathering and is fully explained to the carer.

The first stage is to assist the carer in accepting that the intervention is a joint piece of work. It is important that he understands that he is a valued, informed and engaged colleague of the life story therapist. To this end, I state to carers that they are 'professionals' who have care of traumatized children and so the first thing they need to be aware of is the child's known history. Often I find that carers are told very little about the child they have welcomed into their home. When challenged, social care workers tell me that this is due to the confidentiality of the information held on file. This is perplexing; carers are exposed to the young person 24 hours a day, seven days a week; their family, their friends are also involved, yet they have no clear awareness of the child's background, experiences and potential. Over the years thousands of carers I have spoken with have told me that they did not know about their child's past, that people were not open – and many say, 'If I had known, I would have been able to cope.'

Carers need an opportunity to hear and understand the history of the child in their care. I share the movement boxes and work through each, so that I am sure that the carer has had an opportunity to consider the information and explore his feelings about it, and whether it changes his view, either reinforces his current understanding or aggravates conflict between him and the child in his care. I need to be mindful of how carers cope with the information, whether they are able to hold this, contain the new and respect the child's confidentiality outside the intervention.

It is vital to the process that the carer can accept the information and the thinking generated by this knowledge. The assessment is about whether he can exude confidence and be able to work with information about the child's past, which on occasion can be monstrous, and keep it separate from the present. Life story should be aimed at the past, to reconstruct the 'shards of a child's life' and, once completed, should promote the child's ability to consider the present. It is the child who is encouraged to think about the links between the past and the present. The adult must facilitate, alongside the therapist, and not draw conclusions for the child.

At the end of the three-month information gathering process, and before the beginning of sessions on the life story itself, the therapist needs to be sure that the carer is informed, congruent to the forthcoming intervention, and able to support the child and contain his own enthusiasm. For the carer who is not able to do this, a decision will need to be made by the therapist as to the risks in continuing, or postponing the life story until confidence is evident. In some, less frequent, situations, the carer may be asked to step aside from the work, and the life story therapist may request that another person be involved. In my experience, this has happened on three occasions, and in each case life story therapy was provided with the support of the social worker or session worker involved.

Planning the sessions

The life story therapist needs to ensure that he is able to deliver the life story programme; the direct nature of the work allows a degree of overall planning, which in turn encourages session planning. If the therapist has 400 movement boxes and plans to undertake 20 sessions with the child and carer, he knows that each session needs to cover 20 boxes on average. Ideally he should session plan each therapy meeting and then appraise each in a quality assurance process. Below are examples of a simple session plan and appraisal to assist readers in creating their own.

| Session number: |
| Date: |
| Participants: |
| Location: |
| Time: |

| Aim of session: |

| Risk: |

Figure 5.1 Life story session plan

Were aims met? If not why not?
Evaluation: (To include: Was content pitched to meet the child's level of understanding? What went well? What improvements can we make? Any future recommendations.)
Signed:

Figure 5.2 Life story session outcomes appraisal

The initial session

I tend to provide only two things on my initial visit, these being a pack of coloured pens and a 'Jenga' set (see below). The pens are used for the direct work and recording and 'Jenga' for introduction and assessment. At the initial meeting the child is also presented with the Welcome Book, and I often use an A4 art pad for drawing (more recently an Ipad with a 'doodle application').

'Jenga' (tower blocks)

'Jenga' is a brilliant game for introduction and relationship building. Its very nature is to construct and then deconstruct, only to construct again. Jenga is a tower building game which is fairly affordable, so I'm able to provide a set for each child I work with, at the beginning of the introduction process. Every time I have used it, the results have been very positive.

A typical set will have 54 rectangular bricks, and these are placed in threes to construct a tower which is 18 bricks high. The idea of the game is, carefully, on a turn by turn basis, to remove one brick at a time, using just one hand. Each successfully removed brick is placed on the top of the tower, thus raising the height and leaving the structure a little less stable. The child, the carer and the life story therapist take turns, with the oldest going first. As the process begins I am interested in how each person plays the game: whether the child plays to win, and whether the adult does the same. I am interested in alliances, support, encouragement and engagement, as well as the verbal cues; I am particularly keen to identify the nonverbal cues. As the game becomes increasingly difficult, I hope to observe body language, feeling and emotional expression and tolerance. Built into this, I am also looking for cause-and-effect thinking, planning and strategy. I have always been able to identify the true course of the placement by watching a child and her carer play this game. The interaction and the relationships are fascinating. As an example, I was once playing this game with a mother and daughter, and the daughter, after watching her mother cheat over several attempts, just said, 'If it is that important to win, Mum, then I can always make a mistake.'

The game can help explore feelings of success, anxiety, nervousness and anticipation; each response affords the opportunity to evaluate the communication between those involved. My checklist for consideration is as below:

How do the child and carer:

- assess risk?
- approach the task?
- cope with anticipation?
- manage with pressure and tension?
- encourage, engage and/or play strategically?
- offer support, advice and/or guidance?
- demonstrate relationship and/or allegiance?
- react when successful?
- react when others are successful?
- show empathy?
- react to the possibility of failure?
- react to failure?

Are the child and carer:

- kind, thoughtful and/or caring?
- unkind, thoughtless and/or dismissive?
- able to communicate the feelings that they experience?

Once I am happy that the game has yielded as much information as possible, I ask the child if I might take the game away and add things to it. I then take 20 bricks and write a question on each. Some will be general and others specific to the child and her known history. Questions might include, for example:

- If you had a million pounds, what would you buy?
- What makes you scared?
- What makes you laugh?
- If you had three wishes, what would one of them be?
- Do you dream?

The game is then played again with the carer, child and life story therapist and this time, as the bricks are removed and placed on top of the tower, if there is a question on a brick, then it is read out. The person who pulled the brick from the tower asks the question, and everyone has a chance to reply (including the person who asked the question). I have found that the simple act of sharing information, hearing and being heard is a valuable introduction to the life story process. Many children that I work with are upset if they do not pick a question brick, and at the end of the game they will go through the questions and ask each one. The information gained from this exercise is incredibly valuable, and stark questions, wrapped into a game in this way, can be dealt with in a non-threatening way. I once played this game with a ten-year-old girl and she insisted on telling me the answers to all her questions, which led to clarity that her home was safe, she was scared of the dark, she loved her carer and, if given the chance of three wishes, she would wish for a million more!

This game is played a few times over two or three sessions and then I ask if I can take the game away and add more activities to it. I then colour the ends of 18 bricks red, 18 yellow and 18 blue; these colours can be varied to suit the child. When I bring the Jenga set back, I explain to the carer and the child that the game is now to be played by the child and not by the adults. The adults will be there to encourage the child and be available to her as she plays. They are informed that the colours have rules, and then she is able to play. *Red* means the child can ask a question, *blue* means the adults can ask the child a question and *yellow* means that all present can say how they feel. The one rule for this version of the game is that it lasts ten minutes and is not governed by the rise and fall of the tower. All questions from the child or the adults alike have to be related to the subject of the session only, and not about things outside the session. As an example, if we are discussing the child being removed from her home, the questions must relate to this event. The beauty of this session is that the child becomes the facilitator and can manage the interaction.

Again, I play this game over three sessions so that the child can get used to the process, and in some cases children bring Jenga to further sessions if they feel that it might prove useful.

Games: the importance of play

Games are an essential medium for reaching children, and I use many games to engage and to practise relationships, be they of the storming, forming or norming variety. For some children I work with, it is clear that the best way of engagement is to be very directive in the setting up of the game, the instigation of the rules and observance of the same; for me this is a 'storming' effect, as the child is buffeted into the play.

For other children, the approach needs to be more inclusive, where the rules are discussed and the game play shaped. I would hope that the first child who has been 'stormed' is able to move into a 'forming' mode as the relationship becomes more accepted. After a few sessions there is a 'norming' of the relationship, which brings in confidence, reliability and congruence.

Janet West (1980) writes that play helps a child to:

- develop physical skills
- find out what is 'me' and 'not me'
- understand relationships
- experience and identify emotions
- practise roles
- explore situations
- learn, relax, have *fun*
- act out troublesome issues
- achieve mastery.

- Play is symbolic communication.
- Play acts as a bridge between conscious awareness and emotional experiences.
- In play, children embrace the numinous, the luminous and the practicalities of daily life.

Play does not occur on its own; it is symbolic of who we are, our values, our understanding, thinking and experiences. Important events, important relationships and our understanding of the world we live in all become part of the play dynamic. Children will represent what they perceive in life – be that the roles of parents, carers, doctors, policemen, soldiers or teachers. Often these roles are gender-specific, reflecting the cultural world they live in, but rarely does play enact the actual. Imagination, fantasy, hope and desire, despair and death will be present at the game.

The act of playing is an opportunity to engage, to share, to learn and to achieve; it is not just therapy. When you play with children, helping with construction, creative art, physical activity, communication through enactment, you are entering a form of communication that is full of opportunity and discovery. The game becomes a portal for those involved, as the shared activity ultimately brings down the barriers that often exist between the child and the adult.

Social workers will often state that the best time to talk with a child is in the car, and much the same is true for family support workers and other direct service providers. The fact that other activities are going on allows the child to take more risks as she engages in discussion; as the attention of the adult is diverted away from the direct one-to-one, the child is able to talk, think about and act out how she feels inside.

Think of a game that you most like to play. Why?

- Do you think you are likely to win?
- Do you enjoy the challenge?
- Do you enjoy the social context?
- Do you want to become better through practice?
- Do you enjoy beating other people?
- Do you cheat?

What games do you think children enjoy? Why?

- Have you thought about why they like it?
- What are you like with the game?
- Do they always win?
- Do they enjoy the time with you?
- Do they want to practise more?
- Do they cheat?

I love to play chess – but no one else in my family wants to. In writing this training, I am beginning to understand why: I am likely to win, and I do enjoy beating people – but my family get bored, convinced that I am going to win, and therefore they don't like the game. Also…I cheat!

Games that are successful in work with children who have been traumatized through early life experiences and have low self-esteem include:

- Snap
- Happy Families

- Uno
- Guess Who?
- Frustration
- Ludo.

All these games are fast and activity-based, and the child may succeed or fail. If the child says that she is rubbish at the game, the adult can discuss it, ask how she feels and relate that to other feelings. Fast games like Snap allow the child to consider lots of emotions as she wins and loses. Again, the adult can explore those feelings with the child, and role-model how they feel when the adult loses.

Vocabulary of feelings

It is important for the direct work process that we have the opportunity to think about, identify and experiment with the myriad of feelings that we all have the capacity to experience. I have devised several ways in which to explore feelings through activity-based tasks. Like all tried and tested interventions, they can be used as tools for communication with children.

Charades

I find this activity fun; fun is a very important part of life story therapy, and having played Charades with 500 people on a single occasion as part of an international conference presentation, I can say that it seems to be fun for all kinds of people. Even with the most resistant of children and their carers, the game creates a complex range of feelings, which in turn are acted out and identified (or helpfully misidentified).

Have the child, the carer and yourself think about eight different feelings that have been experienced over the last week, and then write each feeling down on a separate piece of paper, being careful not to show your feeling words to anyone. Once this has been done you should all have eight pieces of paper each; each paper needs to be carefully folded to hide the word, and then all 24 pieces of paper are placed in the centre, before the three players. Each person takes a turn to pick one piece of paper, read the feeling on the paper and then act out the feeling – without speaking. The task for the two watching the 'acting' is to guess what the feeling is being acted out. Be aware of the guesses, as each provides a clue as to the child's and the carer's awareness and understanding of how each emotion is felt and how it is communicated.

Emotional regulation and emotional expression are all vital to the life story process. Being able to see how children and their carers act out feelings has always been helpful, both as a reference point and as a visual, nonverbal opportunity for assessment of how children and carers are coping. For some children, acting can reveal hidden feelings and memories, and often there is an opportunity to consider how these feelings affect us, outside and in. I have observed children acting out 'lonely' and it comes across as 'content' or 'sad', 'anxious' or 'scary'. I have also seen carers act out the same word and children interpret this as 'upset', 'cross' or 'dismissive'.

There is, with all similar exercises, a risk; we have to be thoughtful with the child. It is important that we play *with* the child, and that in the play we share what feelings mean to us. The more open we are in this respect, the more engaged the child becomes. She can make sense of the feeling interpretation that she has relied on within placement, and it is often the case that children will tell their carer when these interpretations have been mistaken. The child can reflect on a feeling that might overwhelm her in the process; this is helpful, if the therapist can support her through this. I have found it helpful to use an A4 art pad in these early stages, to record the feeling and the associated memory. In so doing I demonstrate that it is important to me, and also the ability to hold safely the memory shared. It does not help if the memory is heard and put aside, then the message received by the child is that it is of no interest.

The fun generated by the competitive nature of the game needs to be accompanied by a reward; and for this I often will arrange a small prize, in most cases a chocolate or a colouring book. Once the game has been concluded, and each person has had a chance to act out eight feelings, the next step is to consider some of the times when the feelings have been experienced. In the past I have used a simple grid system and plotted Sunday to Saturday (the week). Then the child, the carer and I think about the week we have just had and plot feelings that we have experienced. To do this we all have a separate colour and produce a graph similar to the one in Figure 5.3 below:

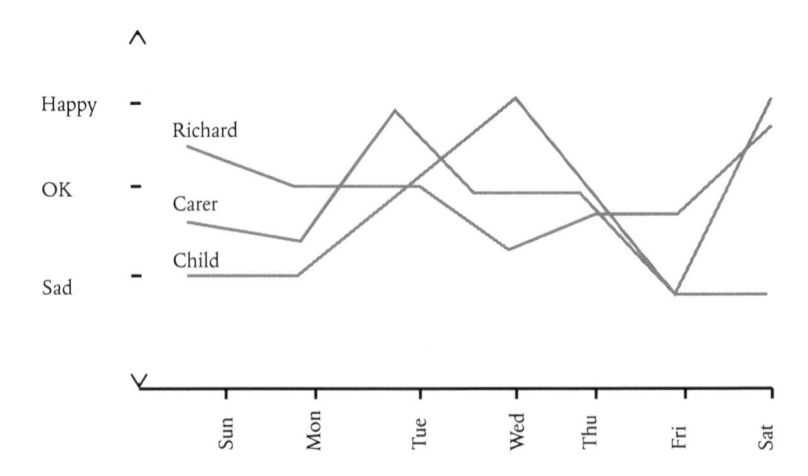

Figure 5.3 Graph showing feelings for a week

You can, of course, add different feelings to the column on the left and a different time scale on the horizontal. What is helpful to the child, the carer and the therapist is that the child can see that we all have feelings, and that sometimes we feel good and sometimes not. Going through the week with the child allows her to think of the reasons why feelings are variable, and the reasons for these feelings, so that we can begin to choose which activities make us feel better and which make us feel worse. In effect, I am beginning to explore ways to help the carer understand the child and the child understand the carer.

'Feelings' theme chart

Using the same feelings list as in the previous activity, this next task provides a legend or key to the life story 'wallpaper' process (see Chapter 7). Together the child, the carer and the therapist base the list of feelings on a topic that produces a symbolic representation of each feeling. The most beneficial way of producing this is to collectively think of a topic that everyone feels would be a fun theme to base the feelings on. Over the years the topics used have included food, shoes, hairstyles, plants and animals, as well as the circus, funfair rides and cars.

The topic establishes the focal point and together, in discussion, the three participants decide which feelings are to be symbolized on that basis. As an example, eight feelings on the theme of 'food' could be:

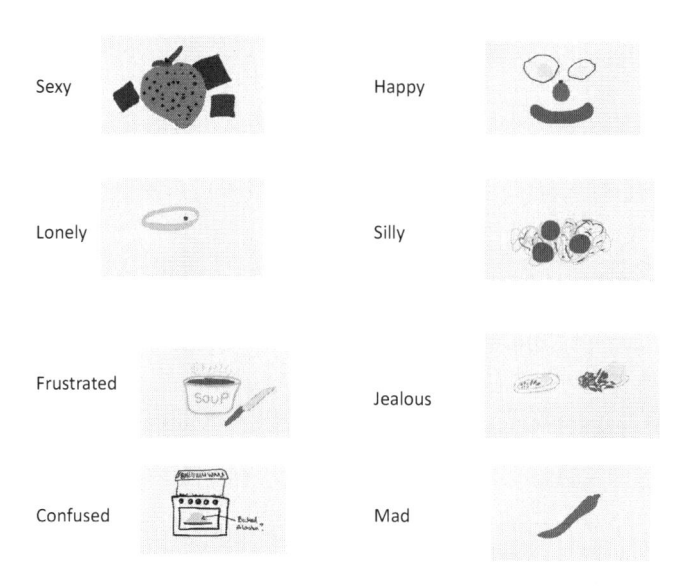

Sexy		Happy	
Lonely		Silly	
Frustrated		Jealous	
Confused		Mad	

Figure 5.4 Feelings symbolized in terms of 'food'

As the feelings are drawn, ideally there is discussion about each one and how they relate to the child's past. (It is important not to relate the feelings to the past of the carer or the therapist, as this exercise is to create the *child's* feelings chart and not the adults'). Once completed, the symbols are photocopied (or digitally photographed). Ideally the therapist makes several copies of each feeling and brings them to the life story sessions once the 'wallpaper work' is introduced (see Chapter 7). With my work, I will often make 20 copies of the feelings listed above, and then I invite the child to pick one feeling at a time when they want me and the carer to understand how things felt, or feel, as we are working through their story.

Children hate being constantly asked how they feel, so the chart allows them to communicate this when they wish to, and the results are very positive. In some cases, the child will seek to use a symbol and decide that it does not reflect what she means by a feeling such as 'angry'. Perhaps the 'angry' that she means is not the right kind of 'angry', so she creates a new symbol for 'very angry' or 'a little angry'. This creates the opportunity to think about different levels of feelings, which adds nuance to the child's range instead of the 'black-and-white' concept that she has, and so she begins to understand the different shades of 'grey'.

'All About Me' books

I am wedded to the concept that the more individual something is, the more value it has. It is for this reason that I do not use the 'All About Me' books that one can purchase from bookshops and various other places.

It is important that children are able to understand their present and feel anchored in a safe port before revisiting the past. Children need to understand that they are safe, that they are owned and cared for by the primary carer. One way that I have achieved this, is by using the process of producing an 'All About Me' book exclusively for the child. This is a PowerPoint production which is designed around the child, exclusive to her and her current placement. The book comes with a disposable camera for the child to take pictures of those things around her that are important to her, and the book is left with her and her carer to complete in a 'two-week' period.

I have completed hundreds of these books and can recommend them as a way to capture the current thinking and feelings of the child who produces it. I was asked to do some work with one child who had been described as emotionally 'empty' (and in one sad note from a previous foster carer as 'the girl with dead eyes'). Having completed the feelings game, the Welcome Book and the feelings chart, it was clear that the child had many valid feelings and was very guarded as to whom she would expose them to. The 'All About Me' book invited her to share her current situation and interest, and what I received was a brilliant representation of who she was. I have detailed some of the questions and responses below as an illustration:

All About Me

My Mum is

She look like this...

I remember these things about my Mum...

Figure 5.5 'All About Me' book

My Dad is

He looks like this…

I remember these things about my Dad …

This is me…

Figure 5.5 'All About Me' book cont.

I have_____brothers and_____sisters.

They are

They look like this

I am living at:

Figure 5.5 'All About Me' book cont.

116 LIFE STORY THERAPY WITH TRAUMATIZED CHILDREN

My hobbies are...

My favourite music is...

My favourite TV programme is...

All about me

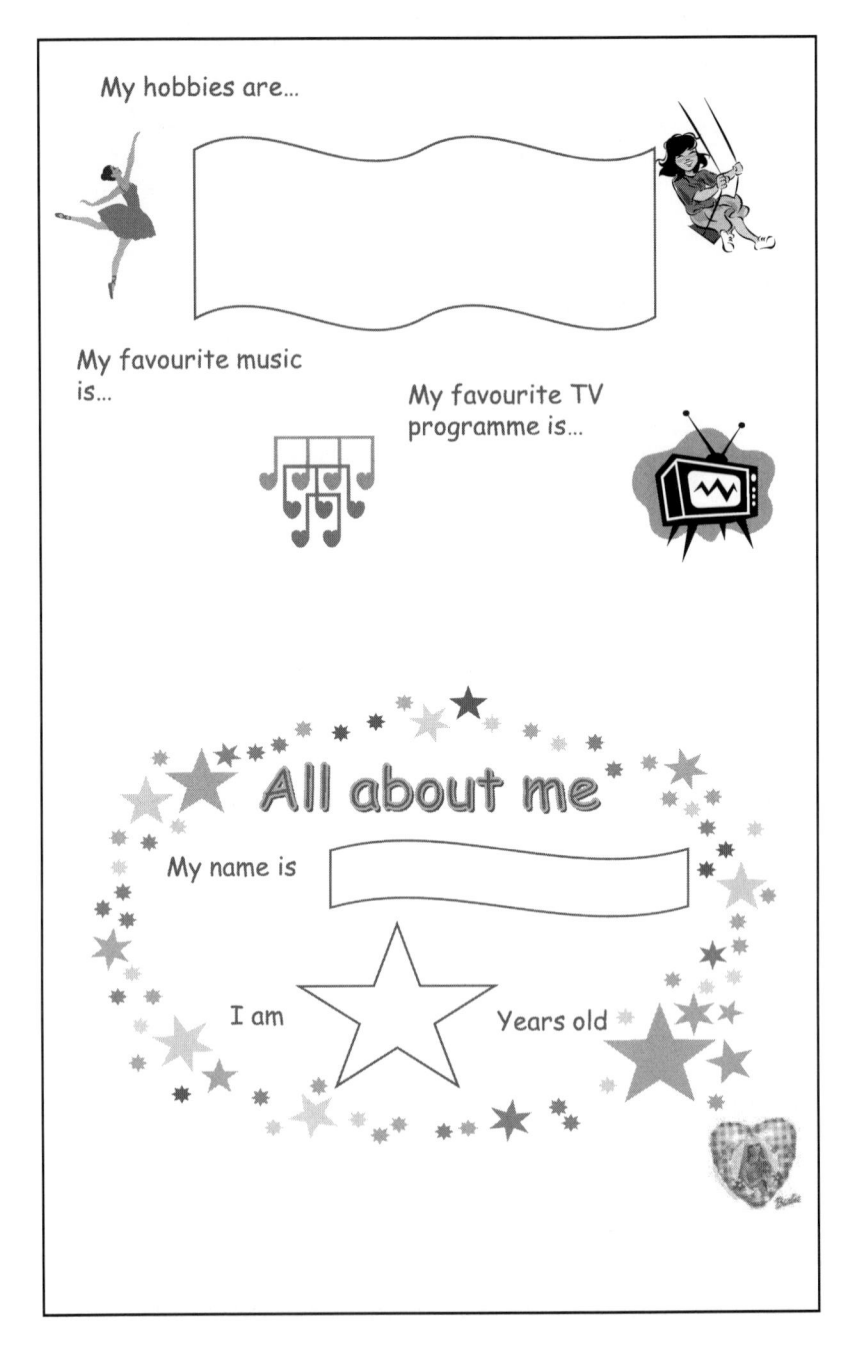

My name is

I am   Years old

Figure 5.5 'AllAbout Me' book cont.

STAGE 2: DIRECT WORK WITH CHILDREN 117

questions

Things that make me sad...

Figure 5.5 'All About Me' book cont.

My school

Things I like about school...

Things I don't like about school...

My teacher's name is:

Things that make me angry...

Figure 5.5 *'All About Me' book cont.*

Once the child has seen her book, she is able to consider the opportunity to have a much larger book which is about her past, and which details how she has come to live where she currently does.

I am always concerned about how we involve children in their reviews and how we assist them to have their voice heard, recorded and responded to. The 'All About Me' book could be used as a six-monthly recording process, which details current developments for the child. It identifies her likes, dislikes, previous placements, contact, feelings about being in care, what she loves, what she hates; her home life, school life, wishes and feelings. Over a typical three-year care period, children would have prepared six 'All About Me' books, showing changes in their interests, their hobbies, their favourite things, their loved ones and so on. Those of us who care for the child also get to witness change, growth, identity formation and – if we do our job properly – recovery.

'Fact, Fiction, Fantasy and Heroism'

When working with children I have found that they are often concerned that they will not be believed, whereas their carers will always be believed, and that it really doesn't matter what they say, because the truth will never be heard.

I considered this over a few years and in 2004 came up with an idea for helping children become free to tell their story without fear or favour. This started with the premise that 'There is no such thing as absolute truth.' I base this on years of experience where my perception of the truth is *my* truth, not necessarily *the* truth. I know from my 'poor' social work in the early 1990s that I rarely recorded the truth. I often recorded what I *thought* was the truth, and when I did record it (as I had the time available), it was based on memory some five (or sometimes more) days after the event. Those of you in social care will know the reality of recording, and understand that we do what we can, but not necessarily at the time we ideally should.

It was with this in mind that I came up with the idea of the 'Fact, Fiction, Fantasy and Heroism' exercise. This has been very useful when working with children about the confusion of life, the 'he said – she said' moments and differing versions of the same event. The role of the therapist is not to interpret, but to facilitate interpretation and exploration, as 'truths and non-truths' are treated as carrying equal weight and affect.

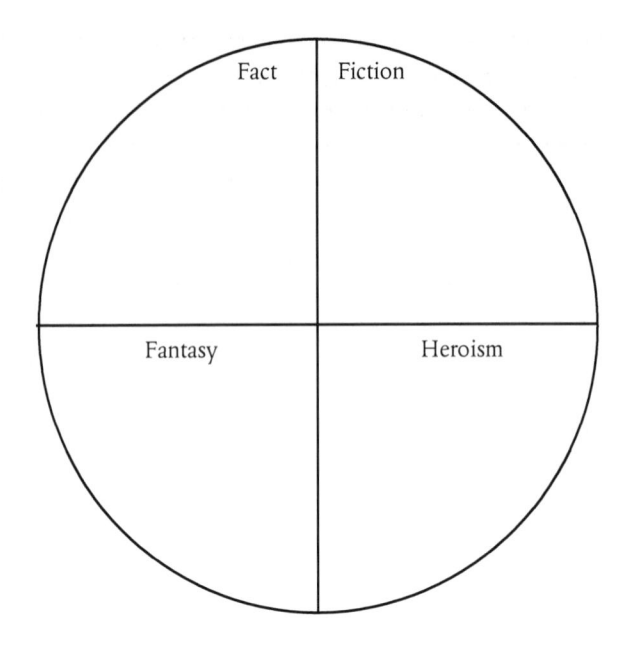

Figure 5.6 'Fact, Fiction, Fantasy and Heroism' template

Ask the child to stand on a large sheet of blank paper, and draw a circle around her, then divide the circle into the four quadrants shown in Figure 5.6. Alternatively, ask the child to lie down on the paper, and draw around her body, then divide the body shape into four sections. Ask the child to consider: what is factual about her; what stories people tell about her; what she wishes could happen; and the people she believes may be able to help her to achieve these things.

Taking the four domains separately, we can explore each concept with the child and the carer.

FACT: WHAT DO WE KNOW ABOUT OURSELVES THAT IS FACT?

We may say that we know when we were born. How? Well, we have a birth certificate with a date on it. We may say we know who our father is. How? 'Well, I was told he is,' 'He looks like me,' and 'He is in all my photographs when I was little.' Birth certificates are only as reliable as the person who completes the paperwork; I have known plenty of occasions when the birth record has proved to be inaccurate, both in name and date – which has a massive impact on the fact of a person's life. We watch soap operas where babies are conceived outside the relationship and nothing is said; we know of DNA tests which confirm that the fathers people thought they had were in reality not their biological fathers.

If you, as a reader, take a moment to recollect your earliest memory. (Often this is a painful one, such as hurting yourself or being separated from your parents, who seemed to have done a 'Hansel and Gretel' on you.) Now, consider how old you were at the time when this memory is located. As an example: my own earliest memory was when I fell off a garden gate and 'cracked' my head open. I was about five at the time! Most of us have a verbal memory at the age of around three to five years. Some have memory recollection aged younger and some aged older than these years. If we take as average four years of age for the first memory, then how do we know the facts of our lives before this time? The simple answer, of course, is through the stories of our parents and relatives and other reference points. Children in the care system may not be able to access this source of information, and consequently may have little understanding of their early lives.

WHAT ABOUT FICTION THEN?

I was born at home in Bristol. My mother, having had two children before me, was very comfortable in labour (so she tells me!). When my time was due to enter into the external world she informed the midwife that she was not going to give birth to me until the credits at the end of her favourite soap opera (called 'Peyton Place'). Sure enough, the credits came at the end of the episode and I was projected out onto a brown paper bag. Now, this is probably not true, but has no doubt been shaped along the years and is a story. But it is my story, something that makes me unique, and so it becomes a truth about me.

We all have stories that make us who we are, and these stories can be dramatic, exciting and worthy of telling, just as other stories not retold, are forgotten and become lost to the teller and the receiver.

How many of us lie? I know I have and will, at times, continue to do so. What is a lie? Is it for good, to protect, to encourage? (Perhaps, in truth, the horse that your six-year-old child has drawn does not look like a horse, but you respond that it is a brilliant picture of a horse). Maybe the lie is to cause harm, avoid, pass the blame (perhaps as an 11-year-old you stole chocolates from your parents, and after eating them, left the wrappers under your sister's bed – enough of confessions, sorry, Liz!). The thing about lies is that, if you tell them long enough and hard enough, they become your truth – a truth that is much more solid than all other truths.

The children that I work with have these kinds of truths, and they are hard to understand, to deconstruct, and in most cases they become unshakeable.

We are, as said earlier in this book, a collection of stories, and it is in the telling of these that we represent who we truly are, how we perceive ourselves, how we see others – and eventually those stories enable us to understand how other people see us.

What about fantasy?

We all fantasize, whether it is about sex, winning the lottery, having a better home, a better job or a better manager, or being the manager (and of course, not being the manager!). Fantasy is a very important part of our truth and who we are, providing us with the opportunity to think beyond our present. I have trained many people from all over the world on life story work and fantasy is an extremely vital part to understand. Without the ability to fantasize, many of our children in care would not survive. Their reality can overwhelm them and so, through fantasy, they create a coping mechanism which allows them to project themselves away from the awfulness of the present. I am sometimes concerned when people state that their child 'lives in a fantasy world', when, in truth, she is demonstrating an ability to manage the chaos and sadness of her reality. I urge carers not to break down this fantasy but to engage with it, understand it and then gently support the child to address it, as they provide safe care and messages of belonging.

> It's by talking nonsense that one gets to the truth! I talk nonsense, therefore I'm human. Not one single truth has ever been arrived at without people first having talked a dozen reams of nonsense, even ten dozen reams of it, and that's an honourable thing in its own way. Talk nonsense to me, by all means, but do it with your own brain, and I shall love you for it. To talk nonsense in one's own way is almost better than to talk a truth that's someone else's; in the first instance you behave like a human being, while in the second you are merely being a parrot. (Dostoevsky 2000)

I worked with a child once who told me that when she lived with her mother she had six white horses in the garden of her home. I knew that she had lived in the middle of a city in a block of flats and that there was no garden where horses could live. I could have said to Michelle, 'Look, this is important work and we do not have time to pretend' and told her that she and her mother lived in a block of flats. Or I could ask her to tell me the horses' names, and whether we could draw them on the art pad. I hope you considered that I would take the second option, and this is what happened. Listening to her fantasy of the horses, their names, which were her favourites and how we could tell them apart, led to my becoming engaged in the fantasy and exploring the story behind it. We later went on a life story journey and visited the places where she had lived before. We arrived outside the flats where she had lived with her mother, and she saw that it was quite neglected and there was no green area where her horses could have lived. I am sure that she thought about the horses. (We had, over the previous two weeks, been walking through her life journey.) On our return, Michelle asked to see her wallpaper and she placed two words in front of her statement about the horses. The sentence on her wallpaper now reads 'I wish I had six white horses.' It is this point that we all try to get to, where a child can align her fantasy with her reality and protect them both.

WHERE ARE THE HEROES?

I often ask carers if they believe that they are heroes to their children, and the majority respond by stating that they are not. Children need their carers to be heroes, to champion them, to claim them, to protect and to love them. Most of us who work in social care understand that we role-model for our children, offering clue sets that we hope they can follow successfully. We all allow our children to infect our lives, we allow our care work to impact on our own families and relationships, and all of us in care work do much more than what we are 'paid' to do. We do this because we want the children that we care for to be valued, to feel worthy and to know that they hold an important place in our thinking and feeling. We cannot expect children to develop a sense of worth if they cannot experience that they are worthy.

USING 'FACT, FICTION, FANTASY AND HEROISM' WITH CHILDREN

After introducing the tool at a conference I was contacted by a social worker who was undertaking life story work with a young boy. Emmeley was happy to contact me to express the positive impact the technique had made on him and the work they were undertaking. With her permission, I present below her feedback on the use of the tool, and specifically on the concept of heroism.

Case study: child 'A'

Having discussed the first three-quarters of the circle, we came to 'Heroes'. 'A' started talking about Ronaldo being his hero, as well as a friend who made 'A' laugh. From this we spoke of his parents and whether they were his heroes. 'A' had said that he didn't want to see them because they had married other people and had other children. He added that he *did* want to see his parents, but only if they were alone and not with his stepmum/dad. When I asked him whether he knew why he did not live with any of his parents, 'A' began to tell his story of how, when he was three years of age, his mother put him in a bin (this was in Somalia). He seemed so shocked by what he had said out loud that he repeated himself. He continued to say that his mum had dumped him where all the rubbish gets dumped, that he wanted to follow her back home but couldn't, and how he knew that he had to get a bus to go home but was unable to. It was his grandmum who came to get him. He asked me why she (his mum) would do that – 'put me in a bin'. We discussed possible reasons, like mental illnesses (depression, breakdown).

I then asked 'A' what happened to him next. He resumed his story by saying that he stayed with his grandmum, then out of the blue he was sent to England to live with his aunt and uncle. He had no idea why he could not live with his grandmum – his preference – and why he was not asked/had no choice in the matter. His time with his aunt and uncle was not good. He was treated blatantly different from his cousins. One particular cousin used to bully 'A' constantly, as did his uncle. 'A' was given secondhand school clothes which were too short in the arms and legs. This gave rise to more bullying at school, 'A' dealt with this by fighting. He got into a lot of fights. Things at his uncle's had become worse and 'A' was taken into care by social services as a result. Although he was not looked after by family, 'A' told me he preferred it in care.

But then after some time his uncle and cousin started to contact 'A' and pester him into telling social services that he had made up the stories about them and they in turn promised things would be better at home. Finally, after a lot of his uncle and cousin harassing 'A', he told social services he made everything up and he went back home to his uncle and aunt's house. The first two weeks he said were okay, then it went back to being how it used to be, but this time 'A' could not go back to social services, which he wanted to do, as he felt they would not believe him after what had happened previously. He spoke about his treatment at his uncle's house, the bullying from his cousin and the isolation he feels. He said if it wasn't for Kids Company he would not have been able to buy the clothes he had on or get the trainers he had on his feet. 'A' sat for a long while reflecting on what he had said and how he felt. I told him that it wasn't his fault, that he was only three years old and that the people who were meant to look after him and keep him safe failed through having/going through their own issues. That he was not to blame for anything, there was nothing he could do, and he was a young child.

'That's what I thought,' 'A' exclaims, 'but I always thought it was me, that I had done something bad.'

For a long, long time he had been carrying a heavy weight, thinking it was his fault why his mum had dumped him, that he had done something wrong. He then said to me, 'Do you know that's why I am how I am now, because of all that stuff that happened.' I tried to put some names to what he went through, for example, abandoned, not wanted, alone, frightened, guilty, helpless, rejected, unloved, etc. It was also important that 'A' understood that all the fighting he was getting into at school was a way of coping with what he was going through in the only way he knew how.

We both sat down for a while. 'A' appeared relieved more than anything, at first it seemed this was the first time he had told his story out loud, so he could hear it for himself. He asked more questions about his mum and I thought about what you said, who could give him those answers. We are still looking into this. 'A' did tell me that his mum is in contact with him and asks him to send her money.

It was so strange how his story unfolded and what he had said earlier when we were talking about what is true and what are stories, how it all tied in with how he felt and what he had experienced.

Emmeley Raphael (Smiler)

Figure 5.7 illustrates the use of the 'Fact, Fiction, Fantasy and Heroism' tool.

Child 'A' above wanted to please his carer by playing musical instruments (although he did not enjoy playing them). He was sad that people were not honest with him, and although he wished to be able to play in a concert, he needed the people around him to assist him.

What is encouraging in Figure 5.7 is that he considers that the people who can help him are his carers and their sons.

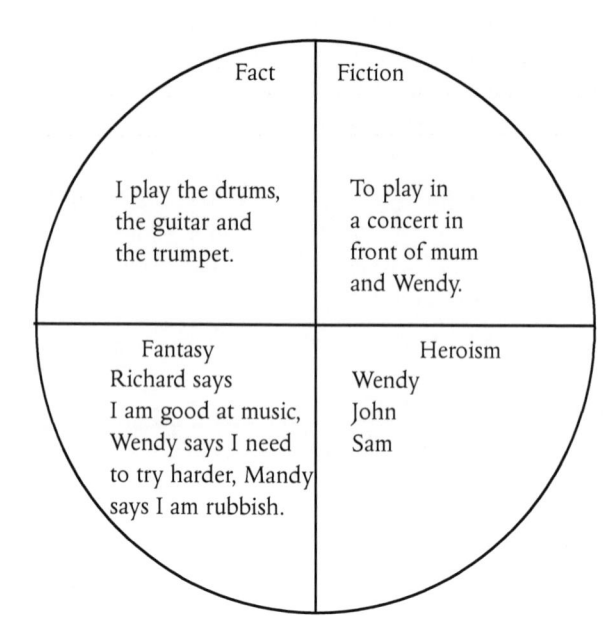

Fact	Fiction
I play the drums, the guitar and the trumpet.	To play in a concert in front of mum and Wendy.
Fantasy Richard says I am good at music, Wendy says I need to try harder, Mandy says I am rubbish.	**Heroism** Wendy John Sam

Figure 5.7 'Fact, Fiction, Fantasy and Heroism': an example

Chapter 6

Stage 3: Understanding the Process

Every so often, children in life story therapy do something that either supports or completely alters the thinking. A 12-year-old child I worked with was struggling with the concept of life story work and why she should tell people what she thought about her life and the people who had played a part in it. I tried all the things that have been covered so far in this book, and none of it actually worked for her. One day Stacey came into the life story session, shouting to me that 'she got it, she got it'. I asked her what she had got, and she explained excitedly that she now understood what life story work was for, and why it made sense for her to do it. She got hold of the paper we were working on (not having started the wallpaper at that point), and drew two bar graphs:

Preoccupation

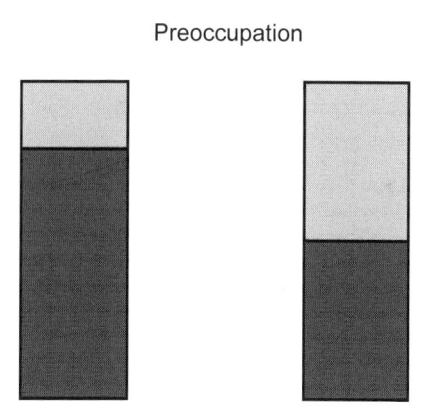

Figure 6.1 Preoccupation

She explained that she was learning about bar graphs at school and during a maths lesson she found herself thinking about her mother and her brother, and whether they were safe. She thought about her abuse, her sadness and that she was having problems with other children in the placement. She was worried about her father and whether he would find her, and concerned that people in the school would find out all about

127

her. I listened and then asked her how she had worked out the life story? She replied that the bar graph had helped her to understand that all the thinking she does, represented in the left-hand column as black, meant that she had little space to try and concentrate on the lesson, or to learn new things, represented by the grey. Stacey then told me that the column on the left was like her, but the column on the right was like another child in class with her, who did not have all the stuff that she thought about going on. That child's black space was not so big, and so she had more space to learn new things and to listen carefully (the grey space). Stacey stated that this was why she was struggling at school and not doing as well as her friend. Again, I said that it sounded really clever to have worked that out, and she replied, 'If I tell you about all the things in my black space, then you can write it down, and we can make sure that it is kept safe'. I agreed that we could do that, and that the wallpaper would make sure that the information was not lost or forgotten and was accessible when it was needed. 'So' she continued, 'if I get to empty what I am thinking all the time, my grey space will increase as my black space gets less'. I was amazed by this reasoning, as Stacey had given a great explanation for preoccupation: if you ever lose something valuable and you cannot remember where you have put it, it begins to invade your normal thought.

Another confession: a few years ago I thought I had left a court report in a hotel room, having remembered putting it in a safe, but not remembering taking it out in the morning. Picture me on a plane travelling to another part of Australia: I suddenly thought, 'Where did I put that report?' All worries about flying, which are constant as I have an unreasonable fear of it, were immediately put to one side. During the following hours I was unable to think of anything but the court paper: 'Where is it? What if someone finds it? What if the court is informed? What about my job?' I was exhausted by the end of this trip – and when I got to my next hotel room, found the court report neatly stored in my luggage bag. The relief was amazing, but it taught me a little about the preoccupation that some of our children have, when they are constantly bombarded with the most traumatizing thoughts and have to try and survive in the world of education and society generally. I would imagine that my bar graph on that plane would have been similar to Stacey's.

I said to Stacey that the aim of life story therapy was to provide the opportunity for her to think about the past, and that this would help her to be more like her friends at school (represented by bar graph on the right). I also said that, if we did our job as well as I would like us to, then I would like to add a new bar graph to her picture.

Preoccupation explained

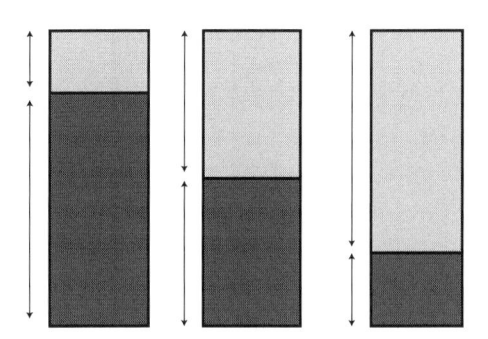

Figure 6.2 Preoccupation explained

I explained that most people find that they can think of several things at once and that the third bar graph means that it is healthy to have some thoughts (healthy memories) that keep us happy and remind us who we are.

As an aside, there is a lot of talk around providing 'level playing fields' for children in care; this has led to the provision of laptops, tuition and other services. None of these would work for children who are traumatized and, as a consequence, they are always at a disadvantage in relation to others. The only way I believe that children can be provided with a 'level playing field' is if we can help them to gain an understanding of their preoccupation, which inhibits their learning opportunities. Life story therapy can provide this. As the children I work with work through their preoccupation, they begin to engage with education, and many of them have gone on to achieve outstanding results in their GCSE and further qualifications.

The Behaviour Tree

I have also developed a version of the 'behaviour tree', which is loosely based on the Tree of Life (Denborough 2008) established by the Dulwich Centre Foundation based in Adelaide, South Australia, and an organization called the REPSSI (Regional Psychosocial Support Initiative), active in South and central Africa. In so doing I also considered the 'damaged goods tree' introduced by Suzanne Sgroi as a useful representation of the affect of the past and how it governs current behaviour. In doing so, I have designed tools which continue to prove highly successful when working with family and foster placement breakdown, behaviour management and, in this instance, understanding ourselves and the roots of who we are.

The Behaviour Tree is particularly useful when working with children struggling in a school environment where there is a breakdown of communication between teachers and the student.

The Tree of Life was introduced as a process of assisting children to make sense of their trauma and the narration around their life journey. It has been used extensively with children who have been affected by HIV/AIDS in South Africa, and is now widely used as a trauma-related identifier in countries such as Russia, Canada and Australia. Children are encouraged to draw their tree, first by visiting their background (the roots) and then moving up the tree to consider their skills and knowledge. The tree encourages children to identify those people who are important to them, protect them and help them to realize their hopes and dreams. The process also promotes group thinking and group healing, whereby groups of children can share their trees and together create a forest of Trees of Life. Through the process of sharing and exploring their differences and similarities, they are also able to draw strength from each other.

Sgroi (1988) introduced the notion of the 'damaged goods syndrome', and based her thinking on her observations of children who had suffered sexual abuse. She identified ten impacts of abuse, which included 'guilt', 'fear', 'inability to trust' and 'pseudo-maturity'. Figure 6.3 demonstrates how the deep-seated effects of abuse can impact on the behaviours of children.

Each of the leaves is clearly detailed as a behaviour, feeling or action that is linked to the branches. Each branch is labelled with an internalized state such as depression, and represents one of Sgroi's ten impacts. The trunk contains the experience of the child and the relationships within the close, extended and the external families. The trunk itself is rooted to the ground, and the roots represent the trauma event and the often hidden factors which are misunderstood, secret and destructive to the self.

Most of the children I work with believe that life story therapy is done because they have been naughty and, as one child told me, because they are 'messed up'. It is important to 'out' these issues as soon as possible, and before the child's own story is explored. By using the Behaviour Tree based on Sgroi (1988) and Denborough (2008) I have found a way in which children, with the support of their carers and the therapist, can consider and develop understanding of their behaviours.

The process

Ask the child to draw leaves at the top of the page. (It is best to use an A1 flipchart for this exercise, and wallpaper if you have started or intend to use this.) It may help if you assist the child in this. Aim for about 15 leaves (Figure 6.3). Once done, consider the different feelings and behaviours, and write each one on a separate leaf. It is helpful to consider positive and/or neutral behaviours as well as those which are more problematic and/or destructive. Then spend a little time talking about the identified issues, and consider the way in which they are shown and the reasons (if any) that the child has for exhibiting them. Reflection works well in this process, and also some mirroring of the carer's and the therapist's own feelings and the reasons why those feelings are present. I also would encourage using speech bubbles (Figure 6.4) to record the responses that seem important, so that there is validation of the exchange.

Figure 6.3 'Behaviour Tree': words on foliage

Some children may struggle with this process, but if you are patient, engaged and attentive, the rewards of letting the child identify her own behaviours are more than worth the time and effort.

Once you have completed the leaves, move to the bottom of the paper. Draw some roots, which should be tangled and plentiful. I would normally have ten roots, but there is no prescribed number.

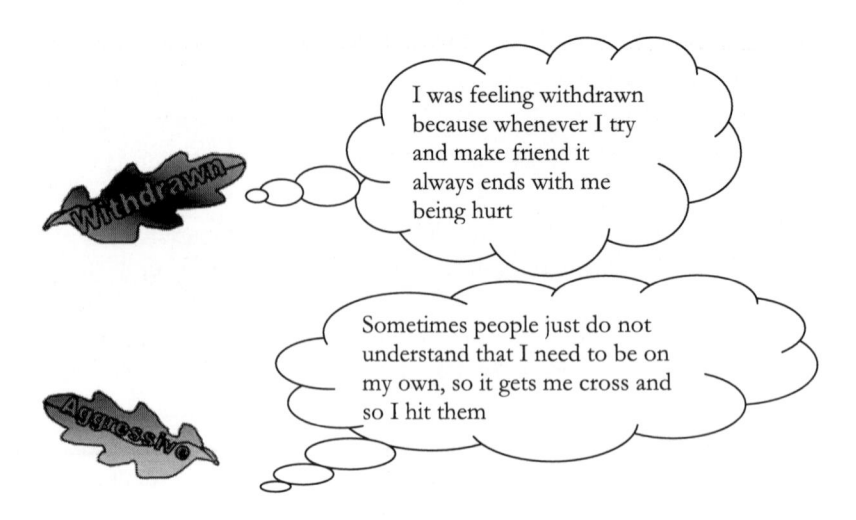

> I was feeling withdrawn because whenever I try and make friend it always ends with me being hurt

Withdrawn

> Sometimes people just do not understand that I need to be on my own, so it gets me cross and so I hit them

Aggressive

Figure 6.4 Leaf and bubble work

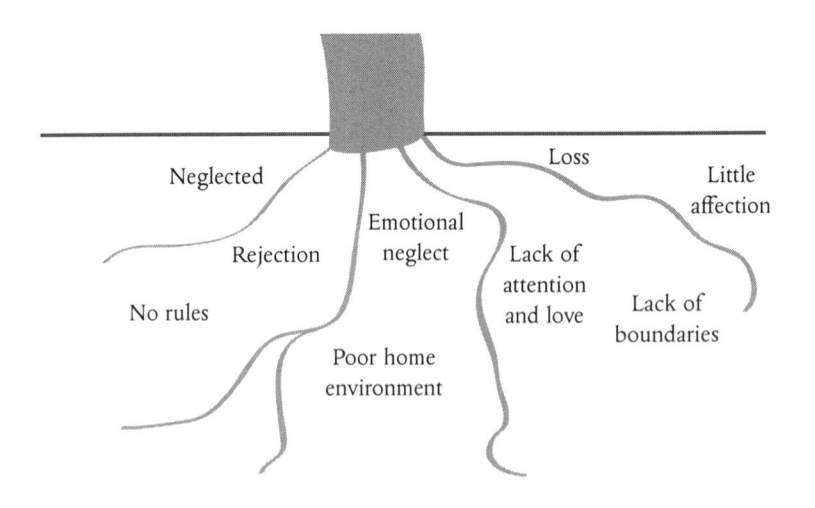

Neglected   Loss   Little affection
Rejection   Emotional neglect   Lack of attention and love
No rules   Poor home environment   Lack of boundaries

Figure 6.5 'Behaviour Tree': the roots

For each root, identify and label one of the issues from the child's past. The carer and the therapist will need to think together about the events, and to ensure that the child understands that they are aware of them and want to help the child to understand the effects of the past. It is most effective if the roots are firmly based in the child's history, and in the history of her family, before she came into care in her current placement.

Sadly, multi-placed children experience repeated trauma within the care system and these injuries are not to be overlooked. For example, a child who has been told that she is going to move to a 'forever family' and then experiences a placement that is far from being that, is likely to have internalized repeated rejection, repeated loss, repeated separation, repeated neglect and ongoing emotional harm.

By identifying the past issues, the carer and the child have an opportunity to consider the reality for the child and to make some sense as to the difficulties within the current placement.

As with all trees, a trunk is needed, and so the carer and the child draw this so as to symbolically link the 'roots' to the present.

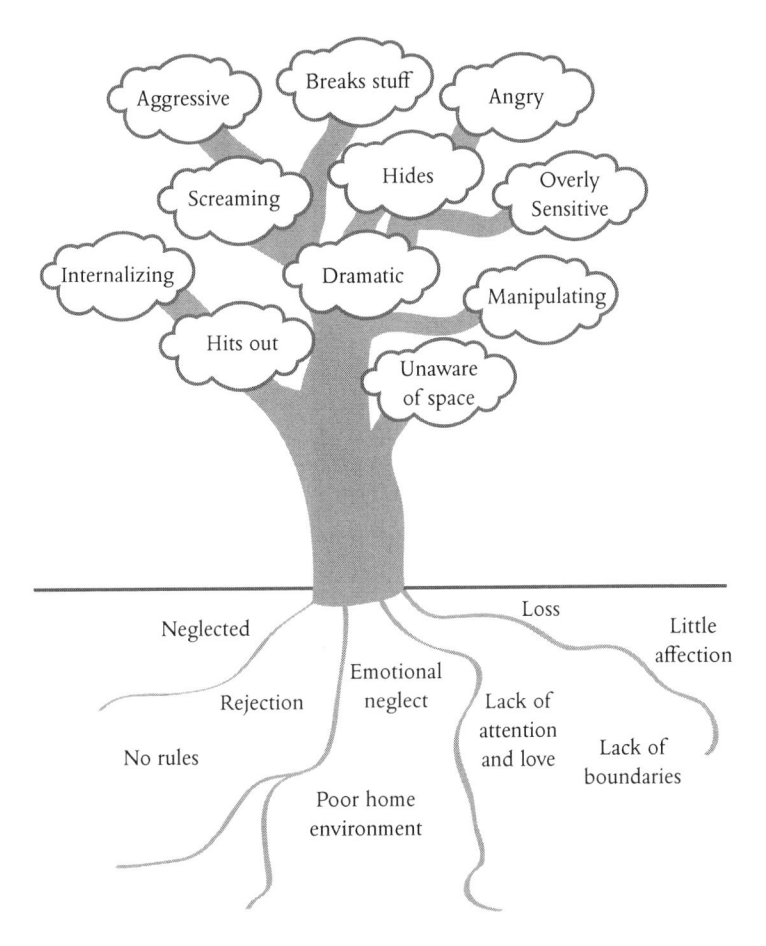

Figure 6.6 The completed 'Behaviour Tree'

The tree is now complete, and the child is encouraged to draw the 'grass' line, which shows that the roots are hidden, often forgotten, and that the leaves are the only visible part of the child. The child and carer can then clearly see that some of the behaviours, feelings and actions are communications from the roots hidden below the ground. Some of the behaviours can be seen as appropriate, if not helpful, for the child. In most cases, the behaviour can be seen as legitimate, and this assists carers to see that the behaviour is not simply chosen to attack, disappoint or reject the carer himself, but merely a learnt, tried and trusted process that keeps the child herself in control (or in some cases, purposefully *out* of control).

The life story therapist can then start to think with the child and the carer about ways in which the behaviour they have identified is helpful or unhelpful. This then leads to a collective thinking about how to protect the behaviours, feelings and actions that are healthy, and how to change those that are not. The therapist needs to discuss how the child uses her behaviours as a form of communication, as well as a defence and coping mechanism. I worked once with a child of 14 who had some very aggressive behaviours and had found himself in a secure environment as a result. We worked on his tree, and as we discussed his roots and then retraced upwards, he stated, 'So my leaves might grow more healthily, and those that are unhelpful and get me into trouble might fall away.'

When working with the potential breakdown of a family placement, this tree exercise has proved to be a placement-saving process. Carers who struggle with the demanding and often confrontational behaviours of their children may feel exhausted and drained by the effort of caring. In some cases they 'give up', as they can see no obvious effect or positive response to their interaction. When working through the tree (on these occasions, without the child present) carers can see that much of the anger, hurt, rejection and verbal aggression presented to them by the child is not about them, and probably never was, but the child's reaction to what the carers represent. The child's internal model and 'shaped by experience' brain installs alerts to the threat of harm, the threat of betrayal, of the unpredictable and the unknown. The more unstable an environment, the more unpredictable it seems, and the stress will result in the child's behaviour becoming more protective, more defensive and more aggressive towards the self and the external representation of the threat, her carers.

> Carers may benefit from understanding that traumatized children are likely to find it difficult to utilize reasoning and logic to modify their behaviour or reactions… Carers can

be supported to understand the purpose and meaning of trauma-based behaviour in children, helping to shift their interpretations away from blame to greater acknowledgement of the ongoing impact of children's abuse experiences. (Mitchell 2008)

An illustration of this occurred recently when I was asked to assess kinship carers who had stepped up to care for their grandson. They were struggling with his behaviour; he was hurting them, their pets and himself. The child had some testing tantrums, which led to him being placed 'on the naughty step' for long periods of time. He had begun to take the behaviour outside the home, and this was causing difficulties with the neighbours. The 'tree' process helped to identify the past experiences that the child had lived through and the legitimacy of some of the behaviours he had adopted. I referred to the importance of providing a secure base, which was as predictable, as consistent and repetitive as possible. It became apparent that the distress and responsibility for the abuse of their grandson weighed heavily on the maternal grandmother's conscience and her perception of guilt. In exploring this and how her behaviour impacted on the care of her grandson and the relationship she had with her husband, she was able to see that the behaviour she was struggling with was in part a reflection of her own trauma.

Good and not so good aspects of life story

There are many concerns about the impact of life story interventions with children, and a helpful way of addressing these can also be a positive way to introduce the next step in the process.

As a threesome, the child, carer and therapist draw a circle at the centre of the paper (wallpaper or A1 flipchart) and then, inside the circle, write 'Things that would be good about doing life story work'. Together identify the reasons why it might be a good thing to do and add these, as shown in Figure 6.7.

Repeat the exercise, but focus instead on the bad things (see Figure 6.8).

Good things about Life Story

- I can find out why I am in care
- Gives a sense of self
- Identity and family
- Special time to think about my family and me
- What, where, when, why, who and how?
- Find out the truth
- Identifying patterns and sequencing
- Who was responsible
- Where are my family now
- Why I am in care

Figure 6.7 Good things about life story

Bad things about Life Story

- You might not like me when you know more about me
- There is not enough information
- It might be retraumatizing
- I cannot ensure that I can see the child when I need to
- My dad and mum will hate me if I talk about what happened
- It can be overwhelming
- It might be disruptive to the placement
- I might not be able to cope
- Its private and I do not want to talk about it
- People will tell lies about me

Figure 6.8 Bad things about life story

This approach will help the child and the carer to express their thoughts about the exploration, and the therapist to consider how each might be addressed in the process. It is best to do this exercise now, rather than at an earlier stage, because the child and the carer have already produced the 'All About Me' document, the games and the feeling chart. Therefore the relationships have been formed and the process clearly identified, with acceptance of the work agreed and contracted. If introduced too near the beginning of life story therapy, worries could derail the process before its start, so timing is important for the success of the intervention. It is essential that the therapist accepts both the good and the bad issues and confirms to the child and the carer that all these can be respected, and that the concerns can be managed and the positives promoted.

Using theory to explain behaviour

Van der Kolk (Streeck-Fischer and Van der Kolk) links the individual's early years experience to the quality of her attachment to the primary carer. The healthier the early experience, the better she is able to draw on her already learnt stress management skills and create techniques that increase her ability to cope with extraordinary life events. The effect of trauma is like an attack on the stress management system, and as the individual experiences stressful event/s and becomes aroused by them, her ability to cope is affected exactly as it was by similar experiences in the past. Van der Kolk identifies that individuals who can calm themselves are able to think and act clearly and cope reasonably well with unexpected events. Those individuals who are unable to remain calm during high-arousal events and in the physical presence of others often have their memory banks triggered.

These triggers are often sensitive signals which indicate danger. The more sensitive and frequent the signals, the greater the perceived danger, and the greater the likelihood that the individual will organize her internal world around the trauma itself.

Movement, the ability to react physically to traumatic events, can have a positive effect in dealing with the effects of trauma. Van der Kolk (2001) states that the effect of trauma on the frontal lobes impairs the individual's ability to think and speak. The ability to plan and to rationalize is reduced, and the natural inhibitors become less effective. Perhaps more interestingly, the individual's ability to speak can be impaired, and when reliving the experience this often is marked by the individual's inability to communicate and to engage in the process of narrative therapy in order to 'move on'. Meanwhile the limbic system (the part of the brain that interprets safety and danger, modulates arousal and deals with sleeping and breathing) can become highly charged. If, as is often the case with children, they are less able to escape physically they can become watchful, frozen, or disassociate from the reality – either way, they 'mentally leave'.

Case study: Gemma

Currently I am working with Gemma, a 13-year-old child who has aggression issues and self-harming behaviour. Most times that I see her she has tales of arguments and fallouts with her school friends and within the foster home. We have been working together, alongside her residential carer for a few months now, and slowly I can see positive change in her self-esteem and her view of the world. Gemma has had a very violent upbringing, her experience of her mother being regularly beaten by her father and her father being regularly beaten by men outside the home. The family had become involved in the use of and the selling of class 'A' drugs and often, when things went wrong, the father would be beaten up in front of his family. As a result of this, the father would assault the mother when his assailants had gone. Gemma had suffered both trauma and neglect, and as such her developing brain has been 'wired' for survival.

Perry (2003) explains that the brain of a healthy developed child should be twice as large in the Cortical and Limbic regions than that of the brain stem and the midbrain. Perry found in his research that young children who had experienced severe trauma had overdeveloped lower regions of the brain. Although the Limbic and Cortical areas were of appropriate size, at times of stress and/or perceived threat the safety and stress responses acted with more impulse; therefore the opportunity for the messages that were received from the spinal cord up to the higher brain functions diminish, and in some cases unable to complete their journey.

This may result in a child being initially "wired" for survival—being impulsive, anxious, acting from instinct instead of reason, and not able to understand or identify his feelings easily. (Perry 1996)

For some time we have spoken of her anger and how this is seemingly her first response system, but it has been hard for her to understand. Thinking around Perry's research on trauma and the brain, I used his familiar model to explain, in the most basic of terms the concept of 'bottom to top' processing.

Blockage from reaching reasoning, cognitive decision making, conscience, balance and response

Thinking Brain

Blockage in this area preventing reflective and relational comparison

Experience Brain

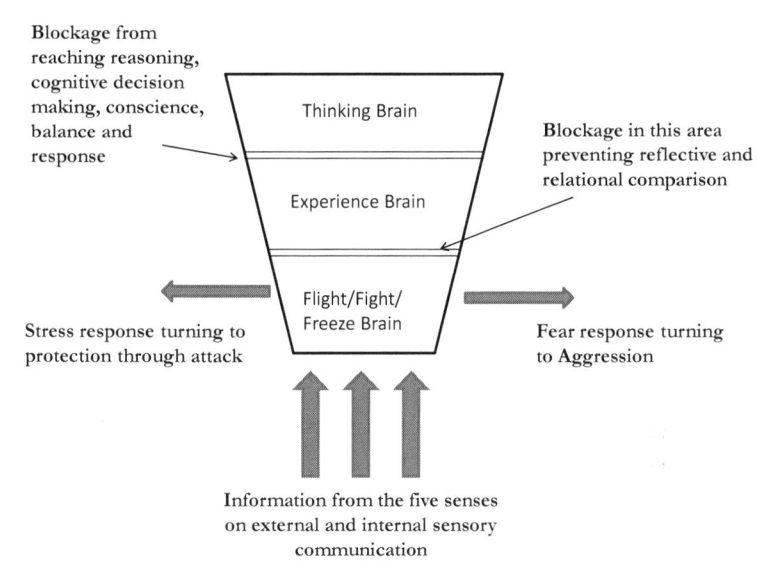

Flight/Fight/Freeze Brain

Stress response turning to protection through attack

Fear response turning to Aggression

Information from the five senses on external and internal sensory communication

Figure 6.9 Fight and flight action

When Abram Kardiner first introduced the concept of Post Traumatic Stress Disorder in 1941 – 'The Traumatic Neuroses of War' he called the trauma a 'psychoneurosis' – a mental disorder which affects the soma and the psyche. He continued his studies and in 1947, Herbert Spiegel and he wrote a second book – 'War, stress and neurotic illness'. Kardiner provided valuable insights on the phenomenology, nosology and treatment of war-related stress, as he studied soldiers who were fixated on their trauma, suffering constriction of their personality functioning and atypical dream life.

Sixty years on, and this concept of somatic trauma therapy has developed, the impact of trauma is the process whereby a person-experiencing trauma internalises these by committing them to memory. These memories are 'banked' containing unprocessed information relating to sight, smell, touch and sound. These experiences can remain locked in these memory banks over a lifetime and can continue to cause harm and inhibit healthy development.

A large number of studies have confirmed that traumatized individuals respond to such stimuli with significant conditioned autonomic reactions, such as heart rate, skin conductance and blood pressure (Van der Kolk 2003)

By using the diagram above, we thought together about her reactive patterns to perceived threats and she began to make connections regarding her impulsive nature in relation to the behaviour she exhibits. We discussed actual incidents of the week before and followed the event, how she felt about the event and how she responded by following the arrows up through the brain picture. On each occasion she stopped at the first level and would say 'I have already blown it by then'.

> Indeed, often they over-read (misinterpret) non-verbal cues-- eye contact means threat, a friendly touch is interpreted as an antecedent to seduction and rape -- accurate in the world they came from but now, hopefully, out of context (Perry 2004)

Gemma then said that her carers had 'held' her in a restraint on the last occasion that she had 'lost it' and that, although she did not like this, she felt quickly calmed and after a while was able to think about what had happened, how it had felt and was able to relate to previous experiences while she was still being held and the carers speaking calmly to her. She then went further and said that, if she could just hold the uncomfortable feelings for a short while, she may be able to stop her reactive impulse. She suggested that she might be able to hold the feeling of safety and calm without having to be held; once she got used to the process and able to care for herself. I spoke about the restraint, and she mentioned that it was like a security that was able to hold her and prevent her normal destructive behaviour. We then talked about the experience of being held and she was clear that the more that she was able to rely on the safety and containment the better she felt and the less aggressive to himself or others. She told me that she did not like hurting people and wanted to find a way to stop. She reasoned that she would not always need to be restrained to help her to think about things; that she might be able to learn to be calm and after a few months she might be able to begin to make friends and keep them!

STAGE 3: UNDERSTANDING THE PROCESS 141

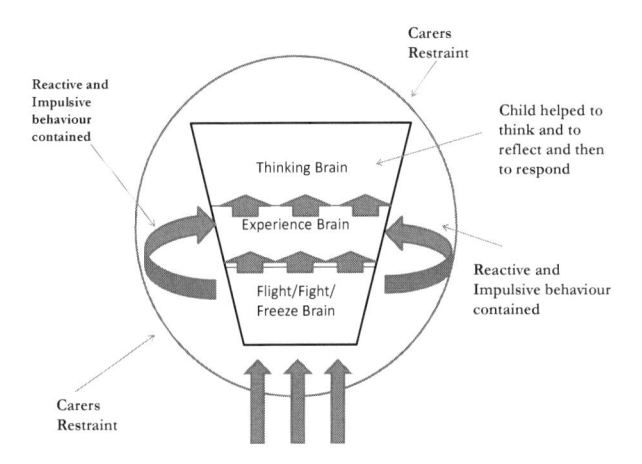

Figure 6.12 Fight and flight contained

The above model does not have to be dependent on physical restraint. In a safe and care based environment, where the adult is present and available, where the child is made aware that they are not alone and are supported, the Carer's restraint is a metaphor for safety and containment. The safer a child feels the more able they are to tolerate their initial responses and able to access their higher level thinking.......the phrase 'stop and count to 10' is a simpler explanation of how we try and control instinctive responses. Her reactive and impulsive behaviours are kept within the boundaries provided by the carer's restraint (safe and secure care); by doing so, there is an opportunity for the child to be supported in experiencing the information she has received and tolerating the instinct to react. This itself, over time, provides the child with the opportunity to engage reflection and to think about the event and to be supported in more healthy responses.

Gemma, her carer and I talked about the experience of being held and she was clear that the more that she was able to rely on the safety and containment the better she felt and the less aggressive her actions were to herself or others. She told me that she did not like hurting people and wanted to find a way to stop. She reasoned that she would not always need to be restrained to help her to think about things; that she might be able to learn to be calm and after a few months she might be able to begin to make friends and keep them!

Chapter 7

Internalization

This chapter describes in practical terms a useful approach for working with children through the 'internalization' stage as described in Chapter 1 (pages 29–31). Over the last 15 years I have used wallpaper as the recording device and extensively discussed this process in *The Child's Own Story*.

The initial recording of the child's story is done, literally, on wallpaper. I use lining paper which is 1000 grade strong. This is relatively inexpensive and easily obtainable from local DIY stores, and thanks to its durability can last for years. (I still use my training example of wallpaper 14 years after it was first completed.) As introduced in Chapter 1, wallpaper is used as a tapestry to paint the journey of the child from their grandparents to the present day. It allows for a visual representation that is chronologically based and produced by all three participants within the therapy.

Unlike computer programmes, scrapbooks, 'fill-in' books and video recording, wallpaper encourages expression of the uniqueness of the child, which is honoured by the process of the recording. The wallpaper can be written on, stuck to, painted on; chalk and pastel work is friendly and is very durable.

Sometimes children do not want to follow the chronological path and so miss out on particular events; this is fine, but when they come to revisit 'their story so far' they identify the missing pieces. The therapist can then cut the wallpaper at the point where the chronology stops, use a new piece of wallpaper to address the missing issues with the child, and then paste it into the main wallpaper work.

Wallpaper becomes the pathway for the child and, at the end of the process, the therapist; the carer and the child can walk along it and ensure that there is a clear understanding of the life story. This internalization allows the child to see the what, the where, the when, the who, the why and the how issues to their life. The intervention and the detail of the people involved are also clear, and the cause and effect, patterns and sequencing become evident and therefore usable.

When introducing wallpaper, it is often good to show an example and then encourage the child to think about the example and how it might be useful. I use training wallpaper from many years ago, that records a story that is true, a little difficult in some areas and funny in others.

The process needs to be fun, and all involved need to be just that – involved.

When explaining wallpaper to children I refer to the Bayeux Tapestry, the 70-metre-long eleventh-century tapestry thought to have been woven by the wives, daughters and lovers of the Norman knights to tell the story of the Norman Conquest of England in 1066 by William the Conqueror. The tapestry tells the story of the Battle of Hastings; but crucially it tells the story of before the battle, during the battle and its aftermath. (You can find out more at www.tapestry-bayeux.com.)

For the children I work with, their wallpaper starts with their extended family and tells the story of their journey right up to their birth. The wallpaper then tells the story up to the child's last placement, and then the final process tells the story of her present and her hopes for her future.

Wallpaper represents the beginning, the middle and the end of the intervention and the 'determined life span' of the therapy, which promotes clarity, evidence and time-orientated concepts that the child, the carer and the therapist can work towards. Important, too, is the fact that wallpaper work is fun: it is full of colour and images. It allows the child, the carer and the therapist to be inventive, creative and imaginative.

Life is a journey and wallpaper allows it to be marked, as one would expect, by dates and events. But wallpaper also allows drawings which are symbolic of journeys to be made along the bottom of the wallpaper. Children choose these themselves – from butterflies and horses to racetracks and bouncing balls, from rivers and canals to aeroplanes. One boy asked for a mountain range as his frieze, symbolizing obstacles which he had overcome. A girl painted her feet, and her footprints decorated the bottom of her wallpaper. (It is important that the frieze of the child's journey is pictured only from the beginning of her life and not that of the parents or grandparents.

As each ball bounces or each butterfly is drawn, a number should be drawn on it to identify the year in the child's chronology. Labelling years in this way will help the reader of the wallpaper to reference the age of the child at the time of the events recorded by her. A good example of this process uses a football team such as Liverpool: at one year of age the child has a picture of a goalkeeper, at two, a picture of a right-back defender, and so on. By looking at the frieze as the wallpaper is unrolled, the child and worker can identify how old she was when, for example, a picture of a house move appears on the wallpaper.

As described in Chapter 5, using the symbols that have been created to represent the feelings that the child has, the therapist can encourage the child to stick these onto the wallpaper. As the child identifies events and attaches meaning and emotional value to these, she can begin to make sense of her external and the internal world. For example, jealous, happy, angry or sexy emotions can be owned by the child, but also fixed to those who have acted within her life. Wallpaper also gives an opportunity for the child to record memories of those events and how others may have felt at the time. One of the earliest life story books I completed included a child's picture of her mother and how sad she was when so many bad things happened when she was a child.

The wallpaper work is direct work, fixed around the child's journey. Each session that the child attends starts with the wallpaper being unrolled and reference made to the previous session. This allows the child and the carer to see immediately what has been achieved and therefore makes it quicker to move forward. Children will often refer to the previous session and add to the wallpaper things that they have thought about, or feel to be important. Also, on occasion, children are shocked by what they have written down and want to remove it because it appears risky. Phil Lawrence, life story therapist at SACCS, recalled how one of his children exclaimed in surprise and unease when they revisited their life story wallpaper with him.

It is important that the wallpaper is completed by the child, with the carer and the therapist taking the chance to engage with and support the child to take the lead. This interaction is essential so that the child can see that her carer is involved and not just a spectator of her life journey: someone who is interested, inquisitive and supportive, in short, becoming attached.

I have been training people to undertake life story work for many years, and the one thing that all seem to find most difficult is starting the process. A few years ago I designed a template for the process and would recommend the following as a way forward.

It is important to start the wallpaper with clarity of purpose. On the first session that you introduce the paper, provide large marker pens and unroll the paper. Ask the carer to draw the child and the child to draw the carer – this often requires encouragement and permission to do the funniest picture possible. As they are drawing, write the date of the start of the process and a brief explanation as to the purpose – 'This is my life story and Richard and Lisa are helping me to find out about me, my life and where I have lived and how I came to live at Lisa's'. Once the pictures have been completed, and, all being well, after the laughs and comments, draw a scroll for each picture and ask the child to write (or offer to write for her) five things that are good about her carer. At the same time, ask the carer to do the same about the child. This exercise is very good for seeing how they value each other, and often each is more interested in what the other has written.

Fact, Fiction, Fantasy and Heroism

Figure 7.1 'Fact, Fiction, Fantasy and Heroes'

The session should then move towards the 'Fact, Fiction, Fantasy and Heroism' work (again, outlined in Chapter 5). If possible, draw around the child's body as she lies on the wallpaper; if she is unsure (or if you are), estimate her shape and draw her on the wallpaper. Once done, divide the shape into four parts and inscribe in them separately: 'What is true about me?' 'What stories do people tell about me?' 'What dreams and hopes do I have?' and finally, 'Who can help me?' Ask the child to fill in the quarters so that she is able to say what is fact, fiction and fantasy, and who her heroes are (Figure 7.1). I have had tremendous results with this exercise as children begin to identify their wishes and feelings, their confusions and their realities. They may need support in doing this work, and as long as you encourage, but not suggest entries, the more effective the outcome will be.

In one session then, the wallpaper is filled for about two metres' length, and the child, the carer and the therapist have all been able to write on the paper and contribute to the story it tells.

Family Tree

The next session should introduce a family tree process, using either a drawing of a typical tree or, for much better results, my own version of a tree. A 'typical tree' approach involves the drawing of a tree with heavy green foliage and then for the child to name the family members, for each of whom an apple is labelled and placed in the tree. The visual process is interesting and the child's understanding of who is in her family should not be questioned at this time. Often, if the child misses out a family member, there is a reason for this, and the inclusion of family members or foster family members is neither wrong nor right. Currently an eight-year-old boy I am working with decided that he did not want apples but wanted to attribute a particular fruit to each member of his family. He also decided that his family included birth and foster parents and siblings who were and are part of his life. His father was an orange, his mother a pear, his foster mother an apple and his foster father a tomato! This was fun, descriptive and led to lots of conversations about the fruit he chose and the fruit he did not. It was also of interest that he would not refer to himself as a fruit. He insisted that he was a monkey – not a chimpanzee as they were too violent, but a monkey, as they were cute but a little naughty.

For some children I introduce family tree work in a different process. The response to the question of who our parents are may be a simple one that does not demand obvious thought – in my case, 'Barbara and Robin'. I have not had to think too hard about them, and when asked about my siblings, it is the same: 'Mandy, Becky, Matthew, David, Lizzie and Kate'. It is a rhyme and as such, I have not had to consider who they are, just their names. This is a technique for all three people involved in the therapy, so ask the carer and the child to draw on wallpaper their skeletal family trees – demonstrate what you want by producing yours first. The skeletal trees need to be for three generations and will look a little like mine in Figure 7.2 below:

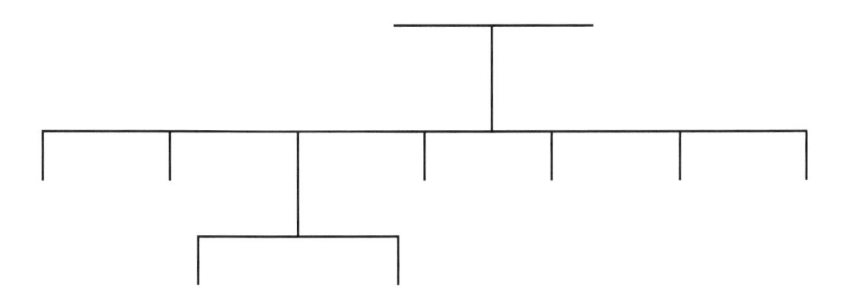

Figure 7.2 Example of a skeletal family tree

The task is for the carer and the child to draw something that reminds them of the people who are in their family. It is important that the therapist (and not the carer) helps the child to draw her family members this is because the carer and the child will need to exchange the stories of their own drawings. As I ask the carer and the child to think about the people on their tree, they have to think about each person, picture them and then either consider or filter out a representation of them. In effect, the person thought about becomes present, which enables discussion and reflection about them. Once the tree has been completed, the therapist can ask about the pictures and the reason for choosing them. A family tree like the one above with 11 people on it, represents 11 stories about me and how I see those I am related to. The information shared is really useful and encourages awareness and attunement between the carer and the child.

If I thought about my mother, I might choose to draw a plate with some food on – I would then hope that the child might ask (and certainly the therapist would ask) why I chose to draw a plate of food. A story would then be told, which would have, like all stories, a beginning, a middle and an end. In this case, as one of seven children living in a small home and having parents who did their very best to provide for us on little income, I recall that there was always an issue around food (the beginning). I remember having a plate of food which contained a very small piece of meat that had shrunk whilst being cooked, a very small potato – and that was it. I was aware of a charity push for the hungry in Sudan and that a television programme was raising money for this. I ran upstairs and grabbed the family camera and took a picture of the plate of food. My mum asked me what I was doing and I replied that I had taken a picture of the food to send to the TV programme so that they might send some of the money raised to us (the middle). My mum was far from impressed and reminded me that the children in Sudan were *really* starving, and sent me off to my bedroom to think about what I had said. Looking back at the 10-year-old I was, I now see, as a 46-year-old, that I was very wrong to have done that, but it was a fair representation of my thinking at the time (the end).

For the task, I have now told those who read this book an awful lot about myself, and if I went on to tell you ten more stories, imagine how much more you would understand about me.

I use this family tree work for all the children that I currently work with, and for children where I am engaged in assessments. At the risk of repeating myself, we are a collection of stories, they are what defines us. To take time to tell the stories, to hear them and to discuss them is therapeutic. For the carer and the child the act of sharing their stories encourages them to become closer and to understand much more about each other.

Over the next few sessions the wallpaper becomes the focus of the intervention, and the details contained within the information bank are slowly worked through. The carer and the child are supported to consider, debate and explore the events of their family life, and as the child begins to understand the lives of her mother, father and siblings, we find that she is also able to consider her own present. There have been numerous occasions when children I have worked with suddenly make 'aha' statements, which are often insightful and become 'healing moments'. One such statement was 'So it wasn't that she did not love me, it was because she didn't know what love was.'

> A major aspect of direct work is listening for the child's perceptions. Until we do this, we won't know if we are to expand their information or correct their misperceptions. (Fahlberg 1994)

The chronology of the child's story will get to her birth and this invites the carer and therapist to mark it with as much information as possible. Birth certificates are essential and, alongside these, weight, height and birth stories are very useful to celebrate. There are times when the birth of the child is central to the success of the life story; I have a child who told me, when I informed her of her birth weight, that she was too heavy. She announced that she was too fat and should have been much lighter, perhaps 1lb instead of the 6lbs 6oz that she was. Her carer stated that she would have been a very poorly baby if she had been that small, and the child replied that she might have died, but it would have been better than 'being the size she I am now'. The carer was shocked by this, but on reflection, the child had given us a real insight into her sense of self and into her body image.

There will be plenty of occasions when children will make statements that will cause concern, and cause a response from the carer which will be an attempt to make the child feel better or worse. It is better, however, to let the child express herself and follow her thinking. In that way, the real issue for the child may surface, and problem solving for the child needs to be held back. I once worked with a child who told me that her father was right to have committed a sex act on her when she was three years old, because if she had not wanted him to, she could have stopped him. An understandable response would have been to tell her that she was not responsible, that her father was wrong to do this and that she had no choice. For a 13-year-old child, this was not the response that she needed. Instead, she needed to be heard, and so I wrote the information down on her wallpaper. I then asked her if she knew what 3-year-olds were like; how big they were, what they could do, how they move, talk and think. She agreed to look with me at a series of books about 3-year-olds, and we looked at child development books to see their abilities. We then, on the wallpaper, wrote down what 3-year-olds are like and we placed a few pictures from the internet. We then thought about dads and what dads are like. She asked me about being a dad and we also spoke with others about their experiences of dads. She then spoke with her carer, and the carer talked about her father, who had died earlier that year. The 13-year-old then put a little about dads on the wallpaper and I placed pictures of dads from the internet next to the smaller (size correct) pictures of the 3-year-olds. She had a sudden 'eureka' moment, she could see it and stated: 'I couldn't have stopped him even if I wanted to!' Although she never stated that he was wrong to have hurt her, she was clear that she wasn't responsible for it.

The wallpaper work continues to tell the story of the child, and as she becomes older on the paper, her own memories will kick in and the connections that she makes will be evidenced on the paper. Over the years people have told me about their abuse, their sadness, their secrets and their lives, and these have been recorded, thought about and 'made sense of'.

The use of thinking cycles is a helpful technique and allows the therapist to think with the child and to consider her choice making, reflection and actions. Thinking cycles can engage children in expanding their information and communication.

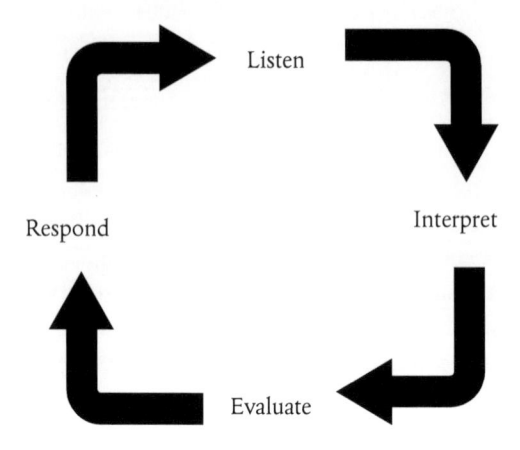

Figure 7.3 The thinking game

The cycle works by thinking through each stage of the communication, therefore resisting the inclination to respond 'on automatic'. Often, when talking with children, adults allow interference to dictate their involvement; children often state that the adults who care for them never listen to them. Most say that the adults would solve their problems, react for the sake of reaction rather than through-thought, and forget the individual and unique nature that each child presents. By following this thinking cycle, the adult can:

- **Listen**: Do not interrupt, shut off the communication or continue to do the hundred other things that need to be done. Listening intently to children involves complete attention. Allow the child to express herself and encourage her nonverbally – by a nod of head, eye contact and open body posture.
- **Interpret**: As the child talks, reflect on what has been shared, explain to the child that the information she have shared is important and that she deserves the time to think though the communication. Consider what lies behind the statement, the way the child verbalized the information, the body language, what was said and what was meant. At this stage the adult can:

- **Evaluate**: Whether the information changes the known issues that the child has, whether the thinking behind the communication is safe or unsafe. The adult can evaluate whether the child needs affirmation, challenge, empathy, direction and/or clarification. Once this takes place, then you can:
- **Respond**: Respond to the child in the best way that assists her to begin her own listening cycle. The response can be detailed, direct or a request for more information. It is important to consider an opportunity to encourage, discourage, comment or conclude.

The thinking cycle looks complex, but it is something that we do all the time. It is an opportunity for the carer and the therapist to think with the child, to reflect on what she is communicating and respond to it. Many children will spend time testing the carer and the therapist, including their ability to cope, respond and give protection, direction, barriers and permission. As the carer and the therapist develop relationships with the child, they have to be mindful that they do not ignore these opportunities to build effective relationships. Avoiding the age-old pitfall of 'problem solving' for children is crucial, as is remembering that high quality care of children is not based on over-protection, thinking and acting for the child. Rather it is the engagement in providing opportunity for children to problem solve for themselves, to think and act responsibly and to realize effective self-protection.

I have used a similar process for reflecting on the actions of others in the past, when considering the information on the wallpaper. The following process has proved immensely helpful for the carer and the child involved. Creating opportunities for children to revisit the boundary demonstrated allows reflection and the idea of change.

- **Recognize an opportunity:** As you work with a child, be open to recognizing times when you can encourage the child to think around her behaviour and the behaviour of others. It is helpful to do this when you have 'space' with the child and her carer – a space that affords time and attention to make the best use of the intervention. Life story therapy should provide these ideal times.

↓

- **Encourage discussion:** Encourage the child to discuss her reaction and how it makes her feel, how it makes you feel, and whether there are more beneficial ways in of demonstrating feelings. Encourage the child to consider how others involved might have felt (but remember to concentrate on the thinking process rather than action).

↓

- **Guide as to when thinking is appropriate and inappropriate:** From the beginning, be open to the child's needs, feelings and emotions; use your knowledge of the child and your relationship to guide/model internal control and external behaviour. This will assist the child to work through distortion and alternative outcomes. If the thinking process is negative, or inappropriate, then be clear that this is indicative of her feelings, and that there are other feelings and areas that might prove more beneficial to consider.

↓

- **Praise and promote self-esteem:** Encourage the child through praise and positive feedback. This promotes self-esteem and positive exchange and provides an invitation for learning and relationship building. It will also allow the child to feel valued and respected, and may encourage her to bring an issue that she will recognize as an opportunity for discussion on the wallpaper.

It is important for carers to encourage children to show their feelings by acknowledging the child's emotions, both overt and covert. Reflecting thoughts that the carer has with the child is a helpful process, commenting on where feelings are felt, how they are coped with and the opportunity to explore where they stem from. Giving a child the opportunity to communicate her feelings by working through her actions and reactions as well as those of others, is essential in developing skills to manage the future.

There are many approaches that are useful within the wallpaper process, and I have detailed a few of these below as communication exercises.

The Mirror of ERISED and the Pensieve Bowl

We are all able to dream, to fantasize, to wish for and to desire. Helping children to think and explore these healthy and, sometimes, unhealthy wishes is an essential task for the life story therapist to undertake. It is the process of this exploration, this unpacking of hope and its difference to expectation, which permits understanding and develops the drive for the child to achieve healthier outlooks. These externalized wishes and feelings can identify much about the child, what they consider to be important and what they see as the difference between an achievable and an unachievable goal. It is the role of the therapist to encourage the child to identify their desire and to illustrate this through play and through art. It is equally important that the child is supported when their expectations are not met and they experience a sense of failure.

By using the recording process explained in the last chapter, the child, the carer and the therapist are able to record this thinking process; by using the wallpaper approach, the child is able to illustrate her thinking, her hopes and her fears. The wallpaper will show her process of thought, the application of her feelings and how these are linked. By understanding connections to the actual, the factual, the fiction and her desires, she is able to separate reality from fantasy, but not lose that essential human quality of hope and dreams.

Many of the children I work with have been brought up in the era of Harry Potter. J.K. Rowling explores Harry's loss of his family and his desire to see them again. By using the context of a mirror (the Mirror of Erised), Harry identifies his loss and separation from his parents. He longs to have them with him and as he looks in the mirror he sees them 'looking back'. This concept of reflecting on his life, his loss and his desire for his parents allows him to begin to accept his situation and to begin to come to terms with his separation.

The mirror appeared in the first book – *Harry Potter and the Philosopher's Stone*. When looking into the Mirror of Erised ('Desire' backwards) Harry saw his greatest wish:

> 'Let me explain. The happiest man on earth would be able to use the Mirror of Erised like a normal mirror, that is, he would look into it and see himself exactly as he is. Does that help?' Harry thought. Then he said slowly, 'It shows us what we want...whatever we want...' 'Yes and no,' said Dumbledore quietly. 'It shows us nothing more or less than the deepest, most desperate desire of our hearts.' (Harry Potter and the Philosopher's Stone – copyright © J.K. Rowling 1997)

Memories and past experiences shape how a child develops, how she learns and how she takes her place in the world. When something traumatic occurs, especially in the early stages of a child's life, it can affect her relationship with her internal and external worlds. It is important for a child to revisit these past events; to have the opportunity to examine each occurrence, to uncover the before, the actual and the after effects. It is the intention of the therapist to assist the child to realize their feelings of shame and guilt. Each occurrence can be overwhelming for the child; it can become invasive, and in itself can prevent other thoughts, feelings and coping strategies from functioning. This overwhelming feeling, affected by distorted memories and fears, needs to be dealt with. To this end, I have used memory boxes: these hold the thoughts, the trauma episodes and the hurt. The memory boxes are drawn on the wallpaper and the child is encouraged to write her worries, confusion and sad memories down. Over the next few sessions the child is urged to select one of the written statements and together we explore the impact of the event, the feeling or the worry. This process provides the opportunity for the child, the carer and the therapist to broaden understanding, explore guilt, and discuss blame in order to identify the role of the child, those involved in the event and those who had responsibility, protection and care of her.

J.K. Rowling (2000) introduced the Pensieve Bowl, which she located in Dumbledore's office. The Pensieve Bowl contains the memories of the headmaster of Hogwarts School, as he is unable to carry all his thoughts and memories within his mind. In the fourth Harry Potter book, Harry explores the Pensieve Bowl and experiences a particular memory of Dumbledore, which in turn allows him to gain a greater understanding of Dumbledore's past. Later in the book, Dumbledore and Harry discuss the Pensieve Bowl:

> Dumbledore: 'I use the Pensieve. One simply siphons the excess thoughts from one's mind, pours them into the basin, and examines them at one's leisure. It becomes easier to spot patterns and links, you understand, when they are in this form.'
>
> Harry: 'You mean...that stuff's your thoughts?'
>
> Dumbledore: 'Certainly.' (Harry Potter and the Goblet of Fire – copyright © J.K. Rowling 2000)

By working through the memories, one by one, the life story therapist is able to consider the perceptions that the child has already developed. In working through the presented perceptions, the therapist can then introduce the perceptions of others (obtained through the information bank collated by the therapist at the first stage of life story).

Memory Jar

In some cases I introduce the 'Memory Jar' process, which is promoted within a solutions-based therapy approach. The Memory Jar uses visual symbolism where children put their memories into a jar using coloured sand. Each colour represents a feeling around the memory (e.g. red sand for a happy memory and yellow sand for a sad memory). The child can write the memory down on corresponding coloured Post-it notes, which are then placed on the underside of the lid. The more memories the child brings to the session, the more sand is put into the jar, and the therapist should encourage plenty of different colours, which will help the child to consider the various feelings that her memories evoke. Once the jar is full, the therapist seals the jar, and then the lid (with all the Post-it notes stuck to the underside) is placed on top and sealed to the jar with more tape.

Air balloon

For some children, the opportunity to detach from the activity that they have experienced is an important process. I have found that the use of an air balloon as a symbolic view of life is helpful for children.

On the wallpaper, draw a hot air balloon and ask the child to draw herself in it. Once she has done that, ask her to draw an adult that she feels close to next to her in the basket. Then ask the child what they can see when they look over the edge of the basket. As they describe what they can see, the carer or the therapist will draw underneath the balloon what the child details. On completion of this, the child is told that the balloon has been blown across to a scarier place, where the wind is strong and the clouds are bursting with rain. The balloon is struggling to float, and then suddenly the wind drops. The child is then asked what they can see over the edge of the basket and this is drawn; often it is a more troubling sight and the child will describe the scene in great detail. The balloon is then gently blown towards the next place and the weather becomes calm and sunny and lots of birds are drawn around the balloon. This done, the child is asked to look over the edge again and asked to describe what they see, and again this is drawn by the carer or the therapist. The balloon then needs to land and the child is asked where they would be prepared to settle with the balloon, and why.

I have used this procedure for children who are struggling in placement (and the carers exposed to their worries). In most cases, the carer realizes that the child is drifting and not able to settle, due to her need to be held safely and loved. This, together with the Behaviour Tree (Chapter 6), helps to shore up placements long enough for me to engage in the more challenging areas and support placements to stability.

The wallpaper process concludes as the chronology meets the present day, and then the child and carer are encouraged to walk the length of the paper and discuss the work, what has been understood and what has not been. This is followed by a little celebration between the carer, the child and the therapist, and then the work is used by the therapist to create the Life Story Book.

The stuck child

The past is something that must be faced. It does not go away, it cannot be avoided. We all have monsters in us, but for some the monsters escape. The past may not always control us, but at times of stress it becomes a very powerful and heavy burden. Life story, similar to other therapies, can only succeed if the child wants you to be involved; much of my time is spent creating relationships for children who have little trust and providing them with opportunities to ask for the service. Other children take part in the process as a means of exploration and because it affords an opportunity for them to ask questions. To these children I offer myself as their private detective who can go away and find out the answers to questions that might be raised. But when those questions evoke painful answers, they may conclude that it is safer to go no further, to seek comfort in the unknown. It is the way in which the therapist's response is given that supports the child and protects her from being upset to the point that she cannot continue the process.

There may be very simple and easily remedied reasons why a child seems to be stuck. For example, she does not 'gel' with (or even like) the worker; or the environment in which the work takes place does not suit her (for example, it is too noisy or too quiet). Then there may be other things happening in the child's life which make life story more difficult than it would otherwise be (for example, the child is going through a bad time in therapy or has had contact with someone from the past who evokes disturbing memories). Again, it may be that someone important to the child, like a foster carer or social worker, is exiting from her life. Or it may just be that the life story worker has not planned the sessions well enough for them to sit well with other parts of the child's life.

There are times when a simple and everyday discussion with the child may reveal that she is not so much stuck as unable to find the words to describe how she feels or what she remembers, or to ask the questions she wants to about events in her life.

Chapter 8
The Life Story Book and Outcomes

As described in Chapter 1, the Life Story Book should represent the work that the child and the carer have completed – whether on wallpaper or on other materials you have used – and should not include any other pieces of information not shared with the child. It should be written to meet the needs and the awareness of the child, and information should be focused on the child's journey and not on others. The child must be able to recognize her work within the book, and the narrative has to be first-person and reflect the child's interpretation of the story of her life.

The first thing to be clear about is the establishment of the roles for creating the book. The therapist is the writer, the carer is the proof reader and the child is the 'editor-in-chief' – and whilst the child does not write her own book, she is the arbiter of what goes in and what stays out. This will include photographs, pictures, information, family trees, memories, letters and art work by the child, the carers and the therapist.

The therapist has to be able to write the book with compassion, forethought and the understanding that the book is the representation of the child's life, so that, the inclusion of court reports, foster care diaries, contemporaneous social care and social worker notes and reports that formed the information bank needs to be carefully considered before any detail finds its way into the book to support the child's own story. The therapist must be sure not to write the book as if he owns the information presented. It is important that any information introduced within the book is accompanied by precursors such as 'the file says', 'my mother told Richard' or 'the court decided'. The therapist must avoid any statement that says, for example: 'Mum was addicted to drugs and then, Richard told me that the social workers should have taken me away.' The therapist should record: 'The social work files state that my mum was addicted to drugs and that the court felt that they should have taken me away when they knew she could not cope.'

With contradictory information, the book should represent both or more points and, if the child has addressed these and decided which one she believes, then this should be highlighted in the book. Many years ago I completed a life story book for a child which detailed the abuse that she suffered at the hands of her stepfather. I had spoken about this to her on a number of occasions, and when it came to writing the book I talked about the abuse and the evidence contained within the social work file. This child left her placement a year or so later and took her book with her. Three years later when she returned to her family home, her parents, and in particular her stepfather, read the book, and he did not react well. It was important that we talked about the abuse, but the stepfather was never convicted of it, the files did not record whether he had or hadn't done it and the records used the word 'abuse' but not 'alleged' throughout. I learnt from this and now use the word 'alleged' if there has been no conviction, and keep the role of the parents to a minimum.

Each book needs to be unique and I still use PowerPoint as the easiest and probably the best software to use for these purposes, as it is more flexible and user-friendly than Word. PowerPoint allows themes, watermarks (which can serve as backdrops to pages, over which text and images can be placed) and lets images appear in the foreground or background. Another advantage of PowerPoint is that it allows the book to be shown on screen as it would appear in book form, so for most children I now provide both a memory stick and a physical Life Story Book. Use a digital camera to take pictures of the wallpaper work and import these into the PowerPoint presentation. In this way you can manipulate the pictures, using crop, positioning and watermarks to enhance the presentation and create an attractive book.

Although the book size is dependent on the work completed on wallpaper, most of the books I have completed have been between 80 and 120 pages in length, which is a good size for children to be able to read and refer to when they need. The book should incorporate the 'All About Me' work that was completed at the beginning of the process, and the theme encapsulated in the 'All About Me' work should flow throughout the Life Story Book to accentuate its uniqueness.

Many children who have completed the books find seeing photographs from the past very upsetting at certain times, so I try to avoid using photographs and instead choose drawings of these people. It is important that we ask children how they feel about the photographs, and whether there are any that they would much rather not have. If this is the case, those photographs need to be placed in the information files and held safely in the life story information box.

As editor-in-chief, the child is sent 6 to 12 pages of the finished draft of her book and provided with a red pen to make changes as she sees fit. We encourage the carer to sit with the child as this happens, so that her decision making can be tested and confirmed. These pages are returned, and then the child is provided with the next 6 to 12 pages, and so on, until the whole book has been reviewed and accepted. If there are areas that the child has decided against, but which the story needs in order to make sense, then I meet with the child to discuss it, but it is the child's choice at the end of the day.

The book must therefore have the work completed by the child, and not be a series of pictures and photographs with little written narration. For younger children, the book should have large, colourful text, and for older children much more information that reflects their thoughts and feelings. It is ideal to use the child's own words as much as possible, and repeating the words adds credence to the voice of the child.

Although in the course of sessions the child may have used words which are not desirable, the book should not echo these, and the language in the book should be sensitive to the readership. The therapist should explain this to the child as he writes the book, and as such, the book should reflect the anger that is felt, rather than the language adopted. There are matters which can be left out of the book, even though they helped the child during the internalization process. These may include, for example, very graphic details of incidents, to which there will nevertheless, be some reference, if not an explicit one.

The book needs to be based on a loose-leaf design, so, once printed, the pages are placed in clear plastic pockets and then placed in a binder folder. This allows the child to decide what to show to whom, and to exercise control over the content of the book. The pages can be numbered and a master copy is kept by the therapist, to ensure that any pages that are mislaid or damaged can be replaced.

Children use their books in many different ways; some for matching processes for new carers, some for relationships when they are older. Other children use their books when they feel recollection of their family dwindling, or when they need to seek comfort. The Life Story Book should be a resource for the child to use to remind her of her journey, and to encourage her to keep adding to it so it becomes a diary of her success and recovery. This personal account can help the child to draw strength from certainty about her past. In the best cases, the Life Story Book becomes a child's passport to the future.

Outcomes

Like many therapies, life story has not been subject to rigorous outcome research. There are various research projects on biographical interventions which mainly concentrate around older people and dementia (Dickinson 1998; Di Terlizzi 1994; Wicks and Whiteford 2003). The current crop of memory centres also takes an interest in enhanced reminiscence therapy, but for children who are traumatized by early abuse the science and research-minded approach is at the beginning of its journey.

Life story therapy needs to install some outcome-based measurement, and to this end I have introduced a version of the SHANARRI approach that I designed with Jill Hughes, family placement team leader in Argyll and Bute (Scotland). 'SHANARRI' is an acronym for the desired outcomes for children living in Scotland: children should be **S**afe, **H**ealthy, **A**ctive, **N**urtured, **A**chieving, **R**espected, **R**esponsible and **I**ncluded. Jill and I decided to design an outcome measurement process, which was then shared with the carers, teachers and social care workers responsible for adopted children living in Argyll and Bute. We designed the following questionnaires, which were sent to all participants.

Key points in the 'SHANARRI' assessment

Safe

It is expected by most parents and carers that children will feel safe at home. Consider the child you are assessing and their current position at home, school and in the community. Think about the impact of past life experiences which have influenced their understanding or feeling of 'safe'. For example, do they flinch when hearing raised voices or when being 'told off' or have done wrong? Are they comfortable enough to make mistakes? Most of the children will be living in a 'safe' environment but where on the line would your child fit?

It is important that you consider the child you are assessing in comparison to a healthy child of similar age in the community. We ask that you use this comparison to help you rate your child on a scale of 1 to 5. If the concerns are acute, we would ask that you score a 1, if the problems are non-existent, then a 5.

As above, we are hoping that you consider evidence to support your scoring, so an example might be:

> 'I have scored John a 2 for this area because he is not able to feel safe in the home; he often hides away from the activities in the house. He has had several restless nights and has not been able to settle. When told off, he withdraws and I notice that he has a wet bed by the following morning. John has told my teenage son that he feels scared in his bedroom at night and is not able to talk about his worries.'

I have considered the area of safety for John and have assessed that he is currently measured at:

. . . .

The assessment evidence for this score is based on the following observations:

. . . .

Healthy

Consider all aspects of health in terms of physical wellbeing and mental health. Are all their health needs being met? When children are accommodated there are often issues around poor dental care or many missed specialist appointments. How far have you managed to catch up if required on any ongoing health needs? Has the child learnt to feel pain or discomfort and allowed themselves to be ill? Some children are so hypervigilant that they have never been ill enough to allow themselves to be comforted. How well do you know the health of your child?

It is important that you consider the child you are assessing in comparison to a healthy child of a similar age in the community. We ask that you use this comparison to help you rate your child on a scale of 1 to 5. If the concerns are acute, we would ask that you score a 1, if the problems are non-existent then a 5.

As above, we are hoping that you consider evidence to support your scoring, so an example might be:

> 'I have scored John a 3 for this area when considering his health and development. He has been relatively healthy whilst in placement but at times becomes pale and is off his food. Food seems to be a powerful control issue for him and this does seem to follow on from contact with his birth family. John has a healthy relationship with his hygiene, although there

are times when he cannot cope with being dirty, this can be obsessive and he has a fear of being dirty due to his previous care where he was punished physically for this.'

I have considered the area of health for John and have assessed that he is currently measured at:

. . . .

The assessment evidence for this score is based on the following observations:

. . . .

Active

Physical activity promotes wellbeing. If we can encourage our children to be active in a positive way it will help their development. How many opportunities does your child get to be active in sports with others or for their own achievement? Learning the rules of a sport, playing in a team, being physically challenged helps self-esteem, as well as avoiding sitting in front of the TV or computer. There is such a range of activities available, your child might not be great at football but might enjoy dancing, swimming or playing a musical instrument. The parent/carer needs to provide the opportunities and encourage involvement even if it means watching a match on a cold, wet afternoon. How much structure is there around your child's active world?

It is important that you consider the child you are assessing in comparison to a healthy child of a similar age in the community. We ask that you use this comparison to help you rate your child on a scale of 1 to 5. If the concerns are acute, we would ask that you score a 1, if the problems are non-existent then a 5.

As above, we are hoping that you consider evidence to support your scoring, so an example might be:

> 'I have scored John a 1 for this area because he is not confident when with other children. He is unable to engage with his peers and often hits out when feeling pressured. The activities that he engages in are dependent on his mood and so he is not able to commit to a club, group or arranged activity. John has been excluded from his youth activity due to sexualized

behaviour and often seeks relationships with adults, which in turn puts him at risk of harm.'

I have considered the area of being active for John and have assessed that he is currently measured at:

....
The assessment evidence for this score is based on the following observations:

....

Nurtured

Most of you have experienced a child playing 'catch up' in respect of being nurtured. Is your child letting you nurture them or are they still keeping you at a distance or even a parenting child? Will they allow you to care about them and love them or are they still at 'arm's length'? This is often an area which is hard to make progress with if the child is already independent when placed. A five- or six-year-old may have had to become much more self-reliant than most children of their age simply because of their early life experience.

It is important that you consider the child you are assessing in comparison to a healthy child of a similar age in the community. We ask that you use this comparison to help you rate your child on a scale of 1 to 5. If the concerns are acute, we would ask that you score a 1, if the problems are not existent then a 5.

As above, we are hoping that you consider evidence to support your scoring, so an example might be:

> 'I have scored John a 2 for this area because he is not able to engage in a nurturing experience. He is quick to reject warmth, choosing to push away attempts to hug him or to offer comfort. John is suspicious of those around him and does not find it easy to express emotions and interact beyond the practical activities in the home. John prefers routine and instruction to natural and integrated approaches. He has distanced himself from those who live with him and seems to need the security of a barrier between him and us to feel safe and accept nurturing care. He has found it very difficult to trust people and will often wait for an instruction rather than act on his own initiative.'

I have considered the area of nurture for John and have assessed that he is currently measured at:

. . . .

The assessment evidence for this score is based on the following observations:

. . . .

Achieving

Not all of us will achieve academically but hopefully we can all find something we can do well at our own level. Children need to get a sense of achievement so they can grow as a confident person. Celebrating achievements and believing in their own ability is the best way of building self-esteem. The challenge is for the child to really develop pride based on their own capability.

It is important that you consider the child you are assessing in comparison to a healthy child of a similar age in the community. We ask that you use this comparison to help you rate your child on a scale of 1 to 5. If the concerns are acute, we would ask that you score a 1, if the problems are not existent then a 5.

As above, we are hoping that you consider evidence to support your scoring, so an example might be:

> 'I have scored John a 1 in this area because he is not able to feel good about himself. He has had great difficulty in his self-belief and has very low self-esteem. John will give up on most challenges that he is faced with, often verbalizing that he is 'useless and what's the point in getting it wrong again'. John has little positive sense of self and as such he finds it impossible to accept praise. When we do try to boost him, he becomes angry, shouts and swears at us and pushes us away. John is content in this negative view of himself and it is this area that we are really struggling.'

I have considered the area of achievement for John and have assessed that he is currently measured at:

. . . .

The assessment evidence for this score is based on the following observations:

. . . .

Respected

How do others view your child? Helping them to understand the world and then translate that into others respecting them as an individual who can function in the world is a challenge. Their view of themselves can be negative and harmful or positive and unrealistic. Promoting a positive self-image is an ongoing task for parents/carers and all those responsible for the child's healthy development.

It is important that you consider the child you are assessing in comparison to a healthy child of a similar age in the community. We ask that you use this comparison to help you rate your child on a scale of 1 to 5. If the concerns are acute, we would ask that you score a 1, if the problems are not existent then a 5.

As above, we are hoping that you consider evidence to support your scoring, so an example might be:

> 'I have scored John a 2 for this area because he has demonstrated respect for some of the people in his life, he is not trusting, but has begun to acknowledge them. Although he has a poor self-image, he is able to relate to others and can be quite jealous of them. It has been difficult for John to accept that people might like him for who he is, and likewise, it takes him considerable time to get on with people and he continues to be suspicious of their motives. John's experience to this point has been that adults let you down and that he is not worthy of their time when adults try to relate to him.'

I have considered the area of respect for John and have assessed that he is currently measured at:

. . . .
The assessment evidence for this score is based on the following observations:

. . . .

Responsible

For a child who has a poor experience of attachment from birth some of the resulting behaviours such as lying and stealing do not lend themselves to a view of the child as responsible. It can take a long period of consistent care to help some children learn to trust and accept responsibility for their own actions. Offering a routine, boundaries and a safe, nurturing environment will help children to understand but it can be a long process. Any opportunity to promote responsible behaviour should be encouraged. Some of the children will have experience of adults who were not able to behave in a responsible manner. These children may need to reshape their understanding before they can become responsible themselves. Where would you put your child on the line?

It is important that you consider the child you are assessing in comparison to a healthy child of a similar age in the community. We ask that you use this comparison to help you rate your child on a scale of 1 to 5. If the concerns are acute, we would ask that you score a 1, if the problems are not existent then a 5.

As above, we are hoping that you consider evidence to support your scoring, so an example might be:

> 'I have scored John a 2 for this area because he finds it difficult to take responsibility for his actions and his behaviours. John often denies that he has done something even though he is seen to do it. He can be exhausting due to his constant denials and will often become aggressive and difficult to keep safe if he feels he is being backed into a corner by us. John believes that he can do what he wants and has little empathy and sympathy for others. John's behaviours can be difficult to understand, challenging and hurtful, following these episodes he acts as though nothing has happened. This can make us, as his carers, very frustrated and affects our ability to be consistent and caring with him.'

I have considered the area of responsibility for John and have assessed that he is currently measured at:

. . . .

The assessment evidence for this score is based on the following observations:

. . . .

Included

It is the aim for all children to be included in their community so they can grow into secure, law-abiding citizens. How much is your child accepted and included in their current peer group? How are they viewed by extended family and friends? It is often difficult for children who have moved around to fit in when their home circumstances may be viewed as different by their friends. This is true of older children moving into placement.

It is important that you consider the child you are assessing in comparison to a healthy child of a similar age in the community. We ask that you use this comparison to help you rate your child on a scale of 1 to 5. If the concerns are acute, we would ask that you score a 1, if the problems are not existent then a 5.

As above, we are hoping that you consider evidence to support your scoring, so an example might be:

> 'I have scored John a 1 for this area because he is not able to engage in activities and episodes with peers without this leading to destructive situations. John finds that the pressure of social interaction is too great for him and so he pushes peers away and finds himself excluded from the activity. He has joined three clubs since being with us, and each has ended in exclusion due to aggressive incidents, as John was unable to enter into intimate relationships or to understand the notion of interaction and becomes defensive as new experiences are presented.'

I have considered the area of inclusion for John and have assessed that he is currently measured at:

. . . .

The assessment evidence for this score is based on the following observations:

. . . .

Once the carer, teacher and social care worker have completed their questionnaires, the results on the quantitative measure can be calculated, and on a simple radial grid a shape is created which represents John in comparison to a healthy child of similar age in the community. A healthy child's score is represented by the circumference of the circle in Figure 8.1. Based on the scoring in the example above, John will occupy the following shape:

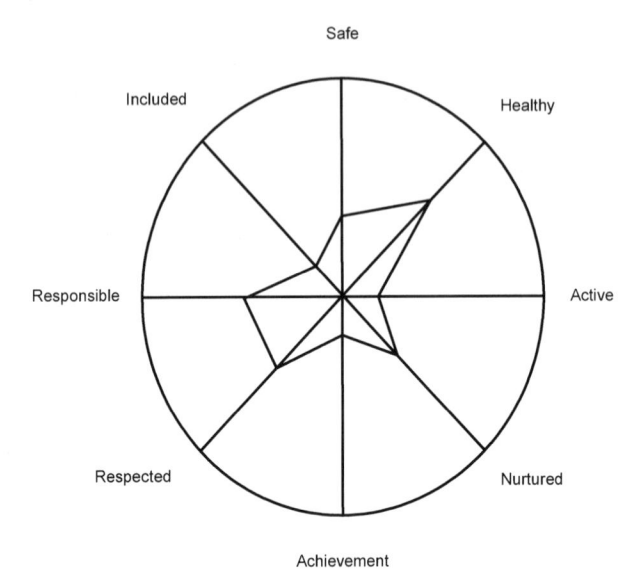

Figure 8.1 Radial grid shape created for John

Using this process to assess your child will help you to consider the areas you might need to work on with her, and to consider approaches which may promote development in a particular area.

The areas of measurement are helpful to the life story intervention, as the therapist is hoping to see that John is able to develop his sense of self, his understanding and learning potential. He is also expecting to see John develop his place amongst his peer and adult contacts and to become positive in his activities and interests. The therapist also works towards supporting the carer to understand and to attune to John and therefore role-model respect and responsibility, so that he can take those clue sets and explore his ability to respect and to be responsible. The use of strengths and difficulty questionnaires is being considered as a way of increasing validation of the assessment, but at the time of writing, as a communication tool the process is beginning to show interesting results.

Chapter 9
Alice: A life story journey

Alice was 11 when she first came to be known by me within the context of life story. She had been presented as a child who had endured sexual assault, exposure to extreme domestic violence, and a child very much alone in the world.

This is not, therefore a story of success, nor of failure, for a moment in her life, Alice was able to meet her family, enjoy her world and experience love, care and belonging. If it were not for the impact of life story though, she would never have had a chance to know herself, to accept the past and feel a sense of belonging.

Alice had two parents that she was aware of: her mother and her father. Her mother is currently an outpatient at a brain injury ward and her father is in prison. She was believed to be an only child and, when placed with her carers, seemed very much alone in the world. There was no social work knowledge of wider family members and it was felt that she would be unlikely to have contact with her family due to their situation.

Information Bank

The first stage of life story is the Information Bank. I arranged to go to her local social services office and read through the files and interview the social workers involved in her care. This was more difficult than I had first imagined; the social work office had recently been relocated and the files archived; the holding social worker was new to the case and, by admission, was playing 'catch up.' I used a template of movement boxes[1] and began to plot the historical movements of Alice through the time she was known by the social services.

Through information gained from files and personnel, I was informed that her parents first came to the attention of the health professionals when her heavily pregnant mother was seen in an emergency ward with facial injuries and a suspected broken arm. The attending medical staff were

---

1   Movement boxes are described in Chapter 4.

informed that Alice's mother had fallen down a few steps and hit her face on the corner of a toolbox. The suspected cause was domestic violence, but no referral was made. A few weeks later, her mother attended the maternity ward and gave birth to Alice. Alice's birth was not complicated and she returned to her mother and father's care after two days. The hospital records informed me that she was born on a particular date in 1998, and that she weighed 7lb 3oz at 2:34 in the morning. I was also able, through maternity records, to confirm that she scored 8 on the Apgar Scale.

Within five days of her birth, the visiting midwife reported concerns for the care of Alice and for her mother. On her visit, the recording indicated possible post-natal depression, but also an observation of bruising around her mother's face. Following on from this early report, the health visitor began to raise concerns for the state of the family accommodation and weight loss of Alice; Alice was eight weeks old at that time. Her mother was reporting feeding problems and eventually Alice was admitted to hospital with failure-to-thrive symptoms.

As I began to note these issues, I was aware of the temptation to second-guess the story. Our need to make sense of situations can often distract us from the individual truth each event presents. Thus we can find ourselves missing vital clues to the history of the child. As an example, if you see failure-to-thrive and signs of post-natal depression and add to this the indication of domestic violence you may assume the presence of neglect and/or rejection and accompanying concerns of 'bonding'. In Alice's case, it was later illustrated in the case assessment notes that Alice's failure to thrive was organic and her mother's presenting post-natal traits were thought to be a reoccurrence of depression that her mother had a history of, but that had not been known about by her general practitioner.

Alice remained in hospital for two weeks and in that times her father and mother separated and, on her discharge from hospital, she returned with her mother, to live with her maternal grandmother.

The recording within the file then jumps to Alice being at nursery, she was three years of age. Records indicated that she was living with her mother and her birth father and that this relationship between the parents had been ongoing for 18 months. There had been a referral to the social services department regarding Alice's behaviour and the nursery staff had concerns for her language (being very coarse) and for her poor social skills displayed within her peer interactions. They had also had concerns for the behaviour of Alice's mother who often appeared with bruising, slurred verbal communication and inappropriate clothing in the inclement weather. There was a recorded discussion with the duty team of the social services, which culminated in a request for an assessment of the family.

Within the file recording I learned that the social worker who responded to the concerns visited the family home and was assaulted physically by the father. Alice's father was subsequently arrested and charged. The social worker recorded that the father had been slurring his words and when she confronted him about his physical state, he had picked up an empty bottle and thrown it at her. This assault was carried out in front of Alice and, according to the report, Alice did not react to the aggressive scene being played out before her.

The police and social services spoke with Alice's mother and it was agreed that she should accompany Alice to the hospital for a check up. There were concerns for Alice's mother that she may herself have been hurt prior to the social work visit. The files record that Alice's mother had four broken ribs and various other injuries that were consistent with a recent 'physical assault', and she was asked to make a statement. Alice's mother refused. It was at this time that the social worker who accompanied Alice and her mother asked Alice if she was OK, Alice replied that 'daddy had hurt her bottom'. With her mother's permission Alice was examined by a paediatrician and evidence of sexual abuse was reported.

Alice was made subject to police protection[2] and admitted onto the children's ward whilst her mother was asked to accompany the police to the police station. The case records then refer to a case conference, the minutes of which informed me that Alice was not able to say how her father had hurt her. Her mother, who denied any knowledge of abuse, stated that Alice's father would never have hurt Alice. She refused to accept that there was a risk to Alice and refused to agree to ask Alice's father to leave the family home. Following the case conference the social workers requested that Alice be placed in the care of a foster carer, this was accepted as the alternative was to be an application for an Emergency Protection Order.[3] Alice was placed with Mr and Mrs Doherty; they were experienced carers who had care of two other children at that time.

Alice continued to be in the care of the Doherty's until she was rehabilitated home eight months later. There was no further action taken

---

2   Police protection in the UK allows the police to remove a child or children to a place of safety and prevent the child or children to be returned for a maximum of 72 hours.
3   An Emergency Protection Order allows the child to be placed in a place of safety for a period of eight days; this can be extended on application for a further seven days. The Order can only be made through the Court.

by the police with regard to Alice's father and he was subject to a risk assessment. The social services, through a case conference, agreed to remove Alice's name from the child protection register and over the next few years the social services began to withdraw from the intervention. There were no further issues to report during this time and the social services closed the case within a year of the initial intervention.

At eight years of age, Alice came back to the notice of the social services when she was found sexually engaged with another child in the toilets at her primary school. This seemed to have alarmed the school and caused Alice to be excluded and a referral to the social services followed. One record indicated the Head Teacher's frustration that Social Services had not supported the school on the three previous episodes of concerns (the social service files did not contain any record of these).

Within four weeks of this report the files detailed investigations at home and Alice was made subject to an Interim Care Order and placed with foster carers in a neighbouring town. Alice told the carer, within a very short period, that her father hurt her mother and that her mother hurt her. Over a few months, Alice began to tell her story and her mother and father were arrested for sexual offences. During this time, Alice began to talk about her brother and sister and how she would like to meet them. According to the social services, she did not have any extended family, and when her parents were asked they refused to give any information.

Sadly, when her parents were bailed pending enquiries, her father attacked her mother and she suffered severe trauma to her brain and was hospitalized. Her father was arrested and convicted of the assault.

Alice was informed of this, the file relates a series of events, which led to her placement breaking down, and reports of sexualized and physical behaviour towards other children. Six placements went by before she stabilized and when she met me, she was settled within a therapeutic foster home. She was 11 years of age.

With this basic historical information, the movement boxes allow the time to examine each fact and to ask questions to enable a better understanding. By considering the eco-maps, which identify the information points, I can begin to piece together Alice's story, and to identify the strands that, once followed, can help me to understand and collate the stories of those involved. I was interested in the 'brother and sister' comment made by Alice. Over many years of doing life story I have found many tens of relatives and these have often provided valuable resources to children. As an example, a respite carer had cared for one child I was involved with. When we interviewed her about her time with the child concerned she expressed interest in finding out if she could support her. This child was placed with the respite carer a year later and the placement became a permanent placement that met the child's need into her adulthood.

As for Alice, I decided to access the birth certificate of her father and her mother. These certificates provided names of their parents, details of addresses when they were born and, through electoral roll registers and people-finding internet sites such as 192.com, I was able to locate the paternal and maternal grandparents. The paternal grandmother lived abroad, and I was fortunate enough to travel to her and speak about her son. This was the breakthrough for Alice.

Her grandmother had care of her sister and brother, and she told me the story of her son and of Alice's mother. They had met in a part of the UK and Alice's mother fell pregnant; during the pregnancy Alice's father got into trouble with the local gangs in the city he lived in. There had been lots of violence and on more than one occasion Alice's grandmother had been told that her son had been killed, only to find out that was not true. At the birth of their second child, the gang was chasing Alice's father and he escaped the country with his wife and two children. They came to live with Alice's grandmother.

We talked a lot more about childhood, and stories for Alice, and it transpired that Alice's dad had been in trouble when he was little and was accused of sexually hurting children. He had managed to run away when he was 19 and that was how he had ended up living in the UK and subsequently meeting Alice's mother. I was told that when the family were living with Alice's grandmother, one of the police officers recognized Alice's father and before the police could come and arrest him, he ran away again, only this time he left the children with his mother. Alice's mother was 'sent for' by her husband once he had settled in another part of the UK and she was told not to bring the children with her. Although Alice's grandmother had not told me, I was made aware that the police advised her to make sure that the children did not return to her son's care. Alice's mother travelled to the UK and when she gave birth to Alice, for all intents and purposes, she was their first child.

Whilst with the paternal grandmother, I met with the children and was allowed to take pictures and record messages from them for their sister. Both wanted to meet Alice and the same sentiments were felt by the extended family.

So, the information bank informed me of previous known history, and gave me the opportunity to discover unknown history and to identify possible resources. There were many other interesting facts obtained, but for the purpose of this case illustration, I will confine discussion to the issues above.

Internalization: Working directly with Alice and her carer

Alice was an inquisitive and lively child who enjoyed being in charge. She was keen to direct the life story sessions and was particularly good with the games we played and the charades. We quickly established rapport and began to develop a common language between Alice, her carer Sara and myself.

The wallpaper work was particularly suited to Alice and, with use of her artistic flare, we began to tell the story of her grandparents and how they had left the UK to live in a sunny place near the sea. We were able to draw on pictures and photographs to think about and consider the truth, the stories, the fantasy and the heroes in her extended family.

Chronologically, we came to the birth of her father and this she was very interested in. We told her of an early life trauma that had happened to him (he had been beaten up by some boys who were indigenous to the country they were living in and they had burnt him). Her father had visible scars on the photograph she had and so explaining the scar was important for her. We talked of his childhood and then we explored the history of her mother and her childhood. The wallpaper journey then introduced how they met, and what had happened. It was at this time that Alice was introduced to the first child they had, her older brother. She was aware of him and said that no one was allowed to mention him. Alice then asked if I knew about her sister and Sara replied that we knew and that I had met them.

As the brother had been introduced into the work, we asked Alice to consider what she would ask of him if she met him. Using a simple scroll picture, Alice began to pose questions that included 'How old are you?' 'Do you know of me?' 'Do you look like me?' and 'Do you like where you live?'. We completed a similar one for her sister and the most telling question she posed was 'Is she prettier than me?'.

The life story work then moved to Alice's birth. There are many techniques that can be used to assist in thinking of the importance of birth. In this instance, Alice's birth details were obtained from the hospital and her early health records held by the health services. We had contacted the hospital of her birth and they had been kind enough to send details, a photograph of the maternity ward and had created a birth tag. As for her weight at birth, it provided an ideal opportunity to consider the vulnerability of a newborn. I recall that we weighed grapes to the weight that she was, with the fruit being delicate; we were able to express how careful we need to be with newborn babies.

Alice continued to work through her life journey, and at significant points, we were able to consider impact, behaviour, choice making and patterns. These activities supported her understanding of the trauma, challenges and decision making of the adults around her. The wallpaper work allows all engaged to rehearse alternatives, to imagine events that may have turned out differently and therefore to attain cause and effect thinking.

Once we arrived at the present day, Alice was able to follow her story across seven wallpaper rolls, about 35 metres in length containing pictures, words, emotions and adventures. We encouraged her to walk along the unrolled paper and interpret her life journey by referencing events and exploring her thinking.

You may recall that I had been successful in identifying the extended family members – it was agreed with the social services that had corporate responsibility for her, that she could travel to meet her family. After 12 years of life, Alice, her siblings, her grandmother and members of the extended family all sat down around a large table and ate together and shared stories and memories.

We concluded the life story work on our return and then developed the book for her to keep as a record of her work. Alice, Sara and I continued to visit her extended family over the next four years and, when she left care, we all hoped that she would go and live with her family in this other country.

So why tell this story? Life story therapy allows children (and adults) the opportunity to regain a sense of self, to follow their life journey and to understand and accept who they are. Alice was able to do just that, to discover who she was, to form new relationships and to experience a loving family. She was able to understand her presenting behaviour, to explore the impact of such behaviour on herself and on others. To learn her value and the values of others and to truly accept that she is lovable, that she can be cared for and that the world, in general, had a place for her.

References

Ainsworth, M.D.S. (1968) 'Object relations, dependency, and attachment: A theoretical review of the infant mother relationship.' *Child Development,* 40, 969–1025.
Applegate, J.S. and Shapiro, J R. (2005) *Neurobiology for Clinical Social Work Theory and Practice.* New York, NY: W.W. Norton and Company.
Archer, C (2003) 'Weft and Warp: Developmental Impact of Trauma and Implications for Healing.' In C. Archer and A. Burnell, (eds) *Trauma, Attachment and Family Permanence: Fear Can Stop You from Loving.* London: Jessica Kingsley Publishers.
Aust, P.H (1981) 'Using the life story book in treatment of children in placement.' *Child Welfare,* 60, 8, 535–536.
Axline, V. (1950) 'Entering the child's world via play experiences.' *Progressive Education,* 27, 68–75.
Backhaus K.A. (1984) 'Life books: Tools for working with children in placement.' *Social Work,* 29, 6, 551–554.
Baldwin, D.C. (1987) 'Some Philosophical and Psychological Contributions to the use of Self in Therapy.' In M. Baldwin and V. Satir (eds) *The Use of Self in Therapy.* New York, NY: The Haworth Press.
Bandura, A. (1977) *Social Learning Theory.* Englewood Cliffs, NJ: Prentice Hall.
Beck, A.T. (1991) *Cognitive Therapy and the Emotional Disorders.* New edition. London: Penguin
Beckett, C. (2002) *Human Growth and Development.* London: Sage Publications Ltd.
Betts B. and Ahmad A. (2003) *My Life Story* CD-ROM. London: British Association for Adoption and Fostering (BAAF).
Bowditch H.P. (1871) 'Über die Eigentümlichkeiten der Reizbarkeit, welche die Muskelfasern des Herzens zeigen. Arbeit aus der physiologischen' (About the property of irritability of the muscle fibres which heart shows: Works from the physiological institute) Anstalt zu Leipzig 6.
Bowlby, J. (1969) *Attachment and Loss. Vol. 1: Attachment.* New York, NY: Basic Books.
Brandt, M. (1999) 'Investigation of play therapy with young children' Doctoral dissertation. University of North Texas.
Bremner, J.D. (2001) 'A biological model for delayed recall of childhood abuse.' *Journal of Aggression, Maltreatment, and Trauma,* 42, 165–168.
Bremner, J.D. (1999) 'Does stress damage the brain?' *Biological Psychiatry* 45, 797–805.
Burnell, A. with Archer, C. (2003) 'Setting up the Loom: Attachment Theory Revisited'. In C. Archer and A. Burnel (eds) *Trauma, Attachment and Family Permanence: Fear Can Stop You From Loving.* London: Jessica Kingsley Publishers.
Camis, J. (2001) *My Life and Me.* London: British Association for Adoption and Fostering (BAAF).
Clark, D.M. (1989) 'Anxiety States. Panic and Generalized Anxiety.' In K. Hawton, P.M. Salkovskis, J. Kirk and D.M. Clark (eds) *Cognitive Behaviour Therapy for Psychiatric Problems. A Practical Guide.* Oxford: Oxford Medical Publications.
Connor T., Sclare I., Dunbar D. and Elliffe J. (1985) 'Making a life story book.' *Adoption and Fostering* 92, 1, 33.
Damasio, A. (1994) *Decartes Error: Emotion, Reason, and the Human Brain.* New York, NY: B.P. Putnam's Sons.
Damasio, A. (1999) *The Feeling of What Happens.* New York, NY: Harcourt, Brace, and Company.
Di Terlizzi, M. (1994) 'Life history: The impact of a changing service provision on an individual with learning disabilities.' *Disability and Society,* 9, 4. 501.
Dickinson, H. (1998) 'Perspectives on Learning Difficulties through Biographies.' In M. Erben, (ed.) *Biography and Education: A Reader.* London: Falmer Press.

Dispensa, J. (2009) *Evolve Your Brain: The Science of Changing Your Mind: Health Communications* (Reprint edition).
Dostoevsky, F.M. (2000) *Crime and Punishment.* (New edition). Ware: Wordsworth Editions Ltd.
Fahlberg, V. (1981) *Helping Children when they Must Move.* Practice series (2nd edition), London: British Agencies for Adoption and Fostering.
Fahlberg, V. (1994) *A Child's Journey through Placement.* London: British Association for Adoption and Fostering (BAAF).
Farrelly-Hansen, M. (2001) *Spiritual and Art Therapy: Living the Connection.* London: Jessica Kingsley Publishers.
Freud, A. (1966) *Normality and Pathology in Childhood: Assessments of Development.* New York, NY: International University Press and London: Hogarth.
Froebel, F. (1903) *The Education of Man.* New York, NY.Glaser, D. (2006) *Understanding Attachment and Attachment Disorders: Theory and Practice.* London: Jessica Kingsley Publishers.
Hardham, V. (1996) 'Embedded and Embodied in the Therapeutic Relationship: Understanding the Therapist's use of the Self Systemically.' In C. Flaskas and A. Perlesz (eds) *The Therapeutic Relationship in Systemic Therapy.* London: Karnac Books.
Hewitt, H. (2008) *Life Story Books for People with Learning Disabilities: A Practical Guide.* Kidderminster: British Institute of Learning Disabilities.
Hill, A. (1945) *Art Versus Illness.* London: George Allen and Unwin.
Hobson, J. (1994) *The Chemistry of Conscious States.* New York, NY: Back Bay Books.
Hughes D.A. (1997) *Facilitating Developmental Attachment: The Road to Emotional Recovery and Behavioral Change in Foster and Adopted Children.* Lanham, MD: Rowman and Littlefield.
Hunter, M. (2001) *Psychotherapy with Young People in Care: Lost and Found.* Hove: Brunner-Routledge.
Huttenlocher, J., Haight, W., Bryk, A., Seltzer, M. and Lyons, T. (1991). 'Early vocabulary growth: Relation to language input and gender.' *Developmental Psychology, 27,* 236-248.
Kardiner, A. (1941) *The Traumatic Neuroses of War.* New York, NY: Paul B. Hoeber.
Kardiner, A. and Spiegel, H. (1947) *War, Stress and Neurotic Illness.* New York, NY: Paul Hoeber.
King, S (2001) *The Shining.* Pocket Book, New York, NY: Simon and Schuster.
King, S. (2002) *The Shining.* New York, NY: Gallery Books.
Klein, M. (1955) 'The psychoanalytical play technique.' *American Journal of Orthopsychiatry* 25, 232–237.
Kot, S. (1995) Intensive play therapy with child witnesses of domestic violence. Unpublished dissertation, University of North Texas, Denton, TX.
Kramer, E. (1975) 'Art and Emptiness: New Problems in Art Education and Art Therapy.' In E. Ulman and P. Dachinger (eds) *Art Therapy in Theory and Practice.* New York, NY: Schocken Books.
Levine, P. and Frederick, A. (1997) *Waking the Tiger: Healing Trauma: The Innate Capacity to Transform Overwhelming Experiences.* Berkeley, CA: North Atlantic Books.
Levitan, I. B., and Kaczmarek, L. K. (1991) *The Neuron: Cell And Molecular Biology.* New York: Oxford University Press.
Levy, M.T. and Orlans, M. (1998) *Attachment Trauma and Healing: Understanding and Treating Attachment Disorder in Children and Families.* Washington DC: AEI Press.
Levy T.M. and Orlans M. (2003) 'Creating and Repairing Attachments in Biological, Foster and Adoptive Families.' In S.M. Johnson and V.E. Whiffen (eds) *Attachment Processes in Couple and Family Therapy.* New York, NY: Guilford Press.
MacLean, P.D. (1952) 'Some psychiatric implications of physiological studies on frontotemporal portion of limbic system ('visceral brain').' *Electroencephalography and Clinical Neuro-physiology.*
MacLean, P.D. (1985a) 'Evolutionary psychiatry and the triune brain.' *Psychological Medicine.* 15, 2, 219–221.
MacLean, P.D. (1985b) 'Brain evolution relating to family, play, and the separation call.' *Archives of General Psychiatry,* 42, 405–417.
Mitchell, J. (2008) 'A Case Study in Attempted Reform in Out of Home Care: A Preliminary Examination of the Introduction of the Circle Therapeutic Foster Care Program in Victoria.' (Master's Thesis). Monash University, Victoria, Australia.
Naumberg, M. (1966) *Dynamically Oriented Art Therapy.* New York, NY: Grune & Stratton.

Nicholls, E. (2005) *The New Life Work Model*. Lyme Regis: Russell House Publishing.

Ogden, P., Minton, K. and Pain, C. (2006) *Trauma and the Body: A Sensorimotor Approach to Psychotherapy* (1st edition). New York, NY: W.W. Norton & Co.

Perry, B.D. (1996) 'Neurodevelopmental Adaptations to Violence: How Children Survive the Intragenerational Vortex of Violence.' In *Violence and Childhood Trauma: Understanding and Responding to the Effects of Violence on Young Children*. Cleveland, OH: Gund Foundation Publishers.

Perry, B.D. (1999a) 'Memories of Fear: How the Brain Stores and Retrieves Physiologic States, Feelings, Behaviours and Thoughts from Traumatic Events.' In J.M. Goodwin and R. Attias, R. (eds) *Splintered Reflections: Images of the Body in Trauma*. New York, NY: Basic Books.

Perry, B.D. (1999b) 'Effects of Traumatic Events on Children.' Interdisciplinary Education Series, 2, 3, Houston, TX: Child Trauma Academy.

Perry, B.D. (1995) 'Childhood trauma, the neurology of adaption and use-dependent development of the brain: How states become traits.' *Infant Mental Health Journal, 16,* 4.

Perry, B.D. (1997) *Incubated in terror: Neurodevelopmental factors in the cycle of violence*. In J. Osofsky (ed.), *Children, Youth and Violence: The search for solutions*. New York, NY: Guilford Press.

Perry, B.D. (2000) 'The Neuroarcheology of Childhood Maltreatment: The Neurodevelopmental Costs of Adverse Childhood Events.' In B. Geffner (ed.) *The Cost of Child Maltreatment: Who Pays? We All Do*. Haworth Press.

Perry, B.D. (2005) 'Maltreatment and the developing child: how early childhood experience shapes child and culture.' In Prasad, N. (2011) 'Using a neurodevelopmental lens when working with children who have experienced maltreatment.' *Research Paper 2,* 8–10.

Perry, B.D. (2006) 'Applying Principles of Neurodevelopment to Clinical Work with Maltreated and Traumatized Children: The Neurosequential Model of Therapeutics.' In N.B. Webb (eds) *Traumatized Youth in Child Welfare*. New York, NY: Guildford Press.

Perry, B.D. (2008) 'Child Maltreatment: A Neurodevelopment Perspective on the Role of Abuse in Psychopathology.' In T.P. Beauchaine and S.P. Hinshaw (eds) *Child and Adolescent Psychopathology*. New York, NY: Wiley.

Perry, B.D. and Hambrick, E.P. (2008) 'The neurosequential model of therapeutics.' *Reclaiming Children and Youth* 17, 38–43.

Perry, B.D. and Pate, J.E. (1994) 'Neurodevelopment and the Psychobiological Roots of Post-traumatic Stress Disorders.' In L.F. Koziol and C.E. Stout (eds) *The Neuropsychology of Mental Illness: A Practical Guide*. Springfield, IL: Charles C Thomas Publishers.

Perry, B.D. and Pollard, R. (1997a) 'Altered brain development following global neglect in early childhood.' Society for Neuroscience: Proceedings from Annual Meeting, New Orleans

Perry, B.D. and Pollard, R. (1997b) 'Homeostasis, stress, trauma and adaption: A neurodevelopment view of childhood trauma.' *Child and Adolescent Psychiatric Clinics of North America* 1, 33–51.

Pietromonaco, P.R. and Barrett, L.F. (2000) 'Attachment theory as an organizing framework across diverse areas of psychology.' *Review of General Psychology* 4, 107–110.

Pointon, C (2004) The future of trauma work: Counseling and Psychotherapy Journal 15(4) Pgs. 10 -13

Ray, D., Bratton, S., Rhine, T. and Jones, L. (2001) 'The effectiveness of play therapy: Responding to the critics.' *International Journal of Play Therapy* 10, 1. 53–83.

Rees, J. (2009). *Life Story Books for Adopted Children: A Family Friendly Approach*. London: Jessica Kingsley Publishers.

Rose, R. and Philpot, T. (2005) *The Child's Own Story: Life Story Work with Traumatized Children*. London: Jessica Kingsley Publishers.

Rowling, J.K. (1998) *Harry Potter and the Philosopher's Stone*. London: Bloomsbury Publishing PLC.

Rowling, J.K. (2000) *Harry Potter and the Goblet of Fire*. London: Bloomsbury Publishing PLC.

Ryan, T. and Walker, R. (1993) *Life Story Work*. London: British Association for Adoption and Fostering (BAAF).

Rymaszewska, J. and Philpot, T. (2005) *Reaching the Vulnerable Child: Therapy with Traumatized Children*. London: Jessica Kingsley Publishers.

Schore, A.N. (1994) *Affect Regulation and the Origin of the Self: The Neurobiology of Emotional Development*. Mahwah, NJ: Erlbaum.

Schore, A.N (2001) *Affect Dysregulation and Disorders of the Self.* New York, NY: WW Norton.
Schore, A.N. (2005) 'Back to Basics: Attachment, Affect, Regulation, and the Developing Right Brain: Linking Developmental Neuroscience to Pediatrics.' *Pediatrics in Review, 26,* 204-217.
Sgroi, S.M. (1981) *Handbook of Clinical Intervention in Child Sexual Abuse.* Lexington Books, Free Press.
Sgroi, S.M. (1988) *Vulnerable Populations: Evaluation and Treatment of Sexually Abused Children and Adult Survivors.* London: Simon and Schuster.
Shah S. and Argent H. (2006) *Life Story Work: What it is and What it Means.* London: British Association for Adoption and Fostering (BAAF).
Shapiro, F. (2001) *Eye Movement Desensitization and Reprocessing: Basic Principles, Protocols and Procedures.* New York, NY: Guilford Press.
Solomon, J. and George, C. (1996) 'Defining the caregiving system: Toward a theory of caregiving.' *Infant Mental Health Journal* 17, 183–197.
Streeck-Fischer, A. and Van der Kolk, B. A. (2000) 'Down will come baby, cradle and all: Diagnostic and therapeutic implications of chronic trauma on child development.' *Australian and New Zealand Journal of Psychiatry, 34,* 6, 903-918.
Suttie, I.D. (1935) *The Origins of Love and Hate.* London: Free Association Books.
Teicher, M.H. (2000) 'Wounds that won't heal: The neurobiology of child abuse.' *Cerebrum* 2, 50–67.
Thomas, D.G., Whitaker, E., Crow, C.D., Little, V., Love, L. *et al.* (1997) 'Event-related potential variability as a measure of information storage in infant development.' *Developmental Neuropsychology,* 13, 205–232.
Usher, J. (1994) *Life Story Work: A Therapeutic Tool for Social Work* (Social Monographs). Norwich: University of East Anglia.
Van der Kolk, B. (1994) *The Body Keeps the Score: Memory and the Evolving Psychobiology.* Boston, MA: Harvard Medical School.
Van der Kolk, B. and d'Andrea, A. (2010) 'Towards a develop-mental trauma disorder diagnosis for childhood interpersonal trauma.' In R. A. Lanius, E. Vermetten, and C. Pain (eds), *The impact of early life trauma on health and disease: The hidden epidemic.* Cambridge: Cambridge University Press.
Walsh, M. (2004) SACCS recovery programme (unpublished)
White, M. (1997) *Narratives of Therapist's Lives.* Adelaide: Dulwich Centre Publications.
Winnicott, D. (1971) *Playing and Reality.* New York, NY: Basic Books.

Internet Accessed Material

www.acrf.org/index.php, accessed on 21 November 2011

www.alexanderyouthnetwork.org, accessed on 30 November 2011

www.attachmentcenter.org/attach, Levy, T.M. (2010) Attachment: Biology, Evolution and Environment, accessed on 10 November 2011

www.bapt.info, accessed on 10 November 2011

www.childtraumaacademy.com/bonding_attachment/lesson01/printing.html, accessed on 23 April 2012.

www.childtrauma.org/ctamaterials/neuroarcheology.asp, accessed on 8 September 2011

www.childtrauma.org/CTAMATERIALS/trau_CAMI.asp, accessed on 8 September 2011

www.childwelfare.gov/pubs/issue_briefs/brain_development/how.cfm

www.dana.org/news/brainhealth, Ackerman, S.J. (2007) The brain in adult life and normal ageing – The Dana Guide, accessed on 8 October 2011

www.developingchild.harvard.edu, accessed on 10 November 2011

www.dulwichcentre.com.au/tree-of-life-australia.html, accessed on 29 October 2011

www.healingresources.info/video_bruceperry.htm, Perry, B. and Winchester, M. (2003) *An Interview with Bruce Perry, Ph.D.*, accessed on 23 April 2012.

www.hedweb.com/bgcharlton/damasioreview.html, accessed on the 8 August, 2011

www.humanorigins.si.edu/evidence/human-fossils/species/australopithecus-afarensis, accessed on 23 April 2012.

www.humanorigins.si.edu/human-characteristics/brains, accessed on 11 November 2011

www.news.bbc.co.uk/1/hi/uk/6167574.stm, accessed on 23 April 2012.

www.oregon.gov/OCCF/hso/index.shtml, accessed on 4 November 2011

www.science.education.nih.gov/supplements/nih4/self/guide/info-brain.htm, National Institute of Health, accessed on 23 April 2012.

www.thinkbody.co.uk/papers/interview-with-allan-s.htm, Shore, A. and Carroll, R. (2001) *An Interview with Allan Schore the 'American Bowlby'*, accessed on 23 April 2012.

www.usnews.com/usnews/culture/articles/961111/archive034966.htm, Brownlee, S. (1996) *The Biology of Soul Murder: Fear can harm a child's brain. Is it reversible?*, accessed on 26th April 2012

www.warwick.ac.uk/fac/soc/shss/courses/pq/specialist_pathway/preparatoryreading/life_story_work_2.pdf, accessed on 5 November 2011

www.zerotothree.org, Perry, B. D. (2000). Traumatized Children: How Childhood Trauma influences brain development, accessed on 10 November 2011

www.zerotothree.org/child-development/brain-development/faqs-on-the-brain.html, accessed on 8 November 2011

Further Reading

Bion, W.R. (1962) *Learning from Experience.* London: Heinemann.
Bowlby, J. (1978) 'Attachment Theory and its Therapeutic Implications.' In S.C. Feinstein and P. L. Giovacchini (eds) *Adolescent Psychiatry: Developmental and Clinical Studies.* Chicago, IL: University of Chicago Press.
Bowlby J. (1988) *A Secure Base: Clinical Applications of Attachment Theory.* London: Routledge.
Bowlby, J. (1982) *Attachment.* New York, NY: Basic Books.
Bowlby, J. and Parkes, C.M. (1970) 'Separation and Loss Within the Family.' In E.J. Anthony and C. Koupernik (eds) *The Child in his Family: International Yearbook of Child Psychiatry and Allied Professions.* New York, NY: Wiley.
Bremner, J.D. (1999) *The Lasting Effects of Psychological Trauma on Memory and the Hippocampus.* New Haven, CT: Yale University School of Medicine.
Cairns, K. (2002) *Attachment, Trauma and Resilience: Therapeutic Caring for Children.* London: British Association for Adoption and Fostering (BAAF).
Chamberlain, D.B. (1981) 'Birth recall in hypnosis.' *Birth Psychology Bulletin*, 2, 14–18.
Chamberlain, D.B. (1987) 'The cognitive newborn: A scientific update.' *The British Journal of Psychotherapy*, 4, 1,30–71.
Chamberlain, D.B. (1988a) 'The significance of birth memories.' *Pre- and Perinatal Psychology Journal*, 2, 4, 136–154.
Cohen, D. (2002) *How the Child's Mind Develops.* Hove: Routledge.
Fonagy P. (2001) *Attachment Theory and Psychoanalysis.* New York, NY: Other Press.
George, C. (1996) 'A representational perspective of child abuse: Internal working models of attachment and caregiving.' *Child Abuse and Neglect*, 20, 411–424.
Gerhardt, S. (2004) *Why Love Matters: How Affection Shapes a Baby's Brain.* Hove: Brunner-Routledge.
Hobson, R.P. (1993) 'Through Feeling and Sight to Self and Symbol.' In U. Neisser (ed.) *The Perceived Self: Ecological and Interpersonal Sources of Self-Knowledge.* New York, NY: Cambridge University Press.
Huttenlocher, P.R. (1984) 'Synapse elimination and plasticity in developing human cerebral cortex.' *American Journal of Mental Deficiency*, 88, 488–496.
Huttenlocher, P.R. (1991) 'Dendritic and synaptic pathology in mental retardation.' *Pediatric Neurology*, 7, 2, 79–85.
Lacher, D., Nichols, T. and May, J. (2005) *Connecting with Kids through Stories – Using Narratives to Facilitate Attachment in Adopted Children.* London: Jessica Kingsley Publishers.
Levine, P. (1992) *The Body as Healer: Transforming Trauma and Anxiety.* Unpublished manuscript.
Levine, P. with Frederick, A. (1997) *Waking the Tiger: Healing Trauma.* Berkeley, CA: North Atlantic Books.
Levitan, I.B. (1991) *The Neuron: Cell and Molecular Biology.* Oxford: Oxford University Press.
MacLean, P.D. (1987) 'The Midline Frontolimbic Cortex and the Evolution of Crying and Laughter.' In E. Perecman (ed.) *The Frontal Lobes Revisited.* Hillsdale, NJ: Erlbaum.
MacLean, P.D. (1990) *The Evolution of the Triune Brain.* New York, NY: Plenum.
MacLean, P.D. (1993) 'Perspectives on Cingulate Cortex in the Limbic System.' In B.A. Vogt and M. Gabriel (eds) *Neurobiology of Cingulate Cortex and Limbic Thalamus.* Boston, MA: Birkhauser.
Maslow, A . (1954) *Motivation and Personality.* New York, NY: Harper.
Perry, B.D. (2001) 'The Neuroarcheology of Childhood Maltreatment: The Neurodevelopment Costs of Adverse Childhood Events.' In B. Geffner (ed.) *The Cost of Maltreatment: Who Pays? We All Do.* San Diego, CA: Family Violence and Sexual Assault Institute.

Perry, B.D. (2001) 'The Neurodevelopmental Impact of Violence in Childhood.' In D. Schetky and E. Benedek (eds) *Textbook of Child and Adolescent Forensic Psychiatry*. Washington, DC: American Psychiatric Press Inc.

Perry, B.D. (2002) 'Childhood experience and the expression of genetic potential: What childhood neglect tells us about nature and nurture.' *Brain and Mind*, 3, 79–100.

Perry, B.D. and Marcellus J.E. (1997) 'The impact of abuse and neglect on the developing brain.' *Colleagues for Children*, 7, 1–4 (Missouri Chapter of the National Committee to Prevent Child Abuse.

Rothschild, B. (2000) *The Body Remembers: The Psychophysiology of Trauma and Trauma Treatment* (Norton Professional Books). New York, NY: W.W. Norton & Co.

Solomon, G. and Siegel, D. (2003) *Healing Trauma: Attachment, Mind, Body and Brain* (1st edition). Norton Series on Interpersonal Neurobiology: New York, NY: W.W. Norton & Co.

Teicher, M.D. (2000) 'Wounds that time won't heal: The neurobiology of child abuse.' *Cerebrum: The Dana Forum on Brain Science*.

Van der Kolk, B.A., Perry, J.C., and Herman, J.L. (1991) 'Childhood origins of self-destructive behavior.' *American Journal of Psychiatry*, 148, 1665–1671.

Ziegler, D. (2002) *Traumatic Experience and the Brain: A Handbook for Understanding and Treating those Traumatized as Children*. Phoenix, AR: Acacia Press.

Subject Index

Page numbers in italics refer to figures.

achievement, assessment of 164–5
activity, assessment of 162–3
'aha'/'eureka' moments 148, 149
air balloon 155–6
Alexander Youth Network 51
'All About Me' books 112, 113–18, 119, 158
animal studies 42
appropriate therapy 19
assessment 19
    carer, and capacity to engage 98–100
    see also information bank
attachment 52–9
    and brain development 37, 44, 55–6
    and physical development 47
    and stress management 137

bar graphs, preoccupations and 127–9
behaviour 66
    learned 49
    using theory to explain 137–41
Behaviour Tree 129–35
birth certificates 29, 83, 120–1, 148
birth details 148–9, 170, 174–5
body language 88, 103, 140, 150
body memory 36–7, 44–8
body movement 46–7
bonding
    pre-natal 55
    see also attachment
boundaries 68, 70, 73
    revisiting 151–2
brain
    and attachment 37, 44, 55–6
    'bottom to top' processing 50, 139, 140, 141
    cognitive representations 47
    development 36, 37–44
    and early life experience 26
    elasticity/plasticity of 39–40, 43–4
    and environment 42–4
    learning and trauma 49–50
    structures and functions 41–2, 46, 51–2, 137–9
    using theory to explain behaviour 137–41
'brain map' 51–2

Care Matters Time for Change 18
care orders 21, 32, 77–9, 172
    Emergency Protection Order 171
carers
    assessment and capacity to engage 98–100
    relationship with child 29–31
    substitute 57–8
    and therapists: wallpaper work 144, 147, 148–9, 151, 153, 174–5
    see also parents
case studies
    Alice 169–74, 169–75
    Britney 32–5
    Callum 21–2
    child 'A' 124–5, *126*
    Gemma 138–41
    Helen 91–2
    Jade 76–9, 80–1, *82*
CENTRE acronym 65
Centre for the Developing Child, Harvard University 56
chaos 66
Charades 108–10
Child and Adolescent Mental Health Service 34
Child Trauma Academy 51–2
Child Welfare Information Gateway 57
Children Act (1989) 21, 32
Children Act (2004) 18
closed questions 89–90
cognitive representations 47
Colombo question 90
Commission for Social Care Inspection 25
communication exercises 108–26, 152–6
confidentiality/privacy 76, 83, 85, 99
contacts, finding 91–4, 173
containment *see* safe environment
contracts 69–70, 73
    interview technique 85–7
'coping style' 49

death certificates 93
deaths 93
development: HIDE principles 64

early life experience 26
early relationships see attachment
ecomaps 81, 82, 83
elasticity/plasticity of brain 39–40, 43–4
electoral roll registers 91–2
Emergency Protection Order 171
emotional dysregulation 46
environment
    and brain 42–4
    HIDE principles 64
    safe 63, 64–5, 66–9, 140–1, 160–1
'eureka'/'aha' moments 148, 149
extended family 124–5
    grandparents 19, 30, 32, 124, 135, 173, 174
    siblings 173, 174, 175
    tracing and contacting 91–2, 173
externalization 29

Fact, Fiction, Fantasy and Heroism exercise 119–23, 145–6
    case study 124–5, *126*
Family Tree 146–9
fear response (flight, fight or freeze) 49, 50
    'bottom to top' processing 139, 140, 141
feelings
    acknowledgement and communication of 68
    communication exercises 108–26
    emotional dysregulation 46
    reflection process 151–2
feelings graph 109–10
feelings theme chart 110–11
free narrative 87–8

games
    Charades 108–10
    and importance of play 105–8
    'Jenga' (tower blocks) 103–5
    'peek-a-boo' 58–9
good and bad aspects of life story 135, 136, 137
good care 66–9
grandparents 19, 30, 32, 124, 135, 173, 174

health assessment 161–2
health and social services processes 169–72
health/medical records 28–9, 169–70, 171, 174–5

healthy/secure and insecure attachment 52–3, 56, 58–9
HIDE principles 63–5
hippocampus 42, 43–4
history
    HIDE principles 64
    life history work 23–6
    parents 30, 34, 173, 174
hypervigilance/arousal 45, 67, 137–8

inclusion, assessment of 167
indigenous peoples 19, 52
information bank 28–9, 30
    access 76, 83
    case studies 76–9, 80–1, *82*, 169–74
    ecomaps 81, *82*, 83
    finding contacts 91–4, 173
    movement boxes 79–81, 94–6, 99
    other uses 94–7
    see also interviews; records
internal working models 52–3, 54, 56, 58
    HIDE principles 64
internalization 29–31
    case study: Alice 174–5
    see also wallpaper work
internet searches 92–3
interviews
    closed questions 89–90
    Colombo question 90
    confirmation 88
    ending 91
    free narrative 87–8
    note-taking 86, 88
    rainbow questions 88–9
    stages 84–7
    summary 90

'Jenga' (tower blocks) 103–5

language
    acquisition 56
    body 88, 103, 140, 150
    life story book 159
learned behaviour 49
life history work 23–6
life journey 31
life story books 32
    format 157–9
    outcomes 160
life story box 93–4
life story therapy 18–21
    definition and approach 26–8
    stages 28–32
listening 27, 84–5, 88, 148, 150–1

Subject Index

medical/health records 28–9, 83, 169–70, 171, 174–5
memory
  body 44–8
  earliest 121
  impact of abuse 43–4
  Mirror of Erised and Pensieve Bowl 152–4
  repetition and 40
  working 47
memory boxes 45, 154
memory jar 155
memory sticks 158
'Memory Store' project 20
Metro Intensive Support Services 20
Mirror of Erised and Pensieve Bowl 152–4
movement, body 46–7
movement boxes 79–81, 94–6, 99
'moving from and moving in' books 25

neglect 57
neurons
  patterns of activation 47
  pruning 39–40
  structure 38
  synapses 38, 39
  types 37–8
neurosequential model 51–2
neurotransmitters 38–9
NIH Massachusetts 26
note-taking at interviews 86, 88
nurture, assessment of 163–4

open questions 87–8
Oregon Commission on Children and Families 28
outcome-based measurement 160–8

parents
  Family Tree 146–9
  history 30, 34, 173, 174
  therapeutic 66–9
  vs child accounts 86
  see also attachment; carers
past and present, relationship between 26–7, 30, 49, 67
'peek-a-boo' 58–9
Pensieve Bowl 154
photographs 158
placements 18–19, 20, 21, 22, 23, 25
  breakdown 57–8
  CENTRE acronym 65
  multiple 24, 58, 77–9, 94–7, 133, 171–3
  saving 134–5, 155–6
plasticity/elasticity of brain 39–40, 43–4

play
  importance of 105–8
  see also games
police protection 171
post traumatic stress disorder (PTSD) 44, 139–40
PowerPoint 112, 158
praise 152
pregnancy, third trimester 55, 56
preoccupations 127–9
privacy/confidentiality 76, 83, 85, 99
'problem solving' 151

rainbow questions 88–9
rapport/relationship building 73, 84–5, 103, 151
records 23–4, 83, 119, 157, 158, 170–1, 172
  birth 29, 83, 120–1, 148–9, 170, 174–5
  medical/health 28–9, 83, 169–70, 171, 174–5
referrals 34, 172
reflection process 151–2
Regional Psychosocial Support Initiative (REPSSI) 129
respect, assessment of 165
responsibility, assessment of 166–7
restraint 140–1
retraumatizing 51
routine 67–8

SACCS 26, 27, 58, 60, 63, 144
safe environment 63, 64–5, 66–9, 140–1, 160–1
school 62
  Behaviour Tree 130
  case study: Britney 32–5
  referral 172
secure and insecure attachment 52–3, 56, 58–9
self-esteem/-image, promoting 152, 162, 164, 165
self-regulation 66
sensorimotor psychotherapy 48
sensorimotor sequencing 36–7, 47–8
sequencing 31
sessions
  initial 103–5
  planning 30, 100, *101*, *102*
Sexual Abuse Child Consultancy Service (SACCS) 26, 27, 58, 60, 63, 144
SHANARRI outcome-based measurement 160–8
siblings 173, 174, 175
somatic markers 47

'spot' work 22–3
story work 21–3
stress
  hypervigilance/arousal 45, 67, 137–8
  management 137
  PTSD 44, 139–40
  trauma and 48–52
  see also fear response (flight, fight or freeze)
stuck child 156
substitute carers and placement breakdown 57–8

therapeutic parents 66–9
therapists
  and carers: wallpaper work 144, 147, 148–9, 151, 153, 174–5
  rapport/relationship building 73, 84–5, 103, 151
  roles and therapy process 60–3
therapy space 60, 63
thinking
  appropriate and inappropriate 152
  cognitive representations 47
  cycles 150–2
trauma 48–52

wallpaper work 30–1, 110, 123, 142–5
  communication exercises 152–6
  Fact, Fiction, Fantasy and Heroism exercise 145–6
  Family Tree 146–9
  reflection process 151–2
  see also internalization
water analogy: attachment theory 55, 56, 57–9
Welcome Book 70, 71–2

Zero to Three 39

Author Index

Ackerman, S.J. 39
Ainsworth, M.D.S. 54
Archer, C. 53
Aust, P.H. 23

Backhaus, K.A. 23
Baldwin, D.C. 61
Bandura, A. 49
Barrett, L.F. 54
Beckett, C. 56, 57
Bowlby, J. 52, 53, 59
Bremner, J.D. 43–4
Brownlee, S. 43–4
Burnell, A. 53

Cameron, D. 54
Carroll, R. 53, 59
Chamberlain, D.B. 44
Charlton, B.G. 47
Connor, T. 32

Damasio, A. 47
d'Andrea, A. 46
Denborough, D. 129, 130
Di Terlizzi, M. 160
Dickinson, H. 160
Dispensa, J. 40
Docker-Drysdale, B. 53, 54
Dostoevsky, F.M. 122

Fahlberg, V. 18, 23, 27, 148
Freud, A. 53

George, C. 53
Glaser, D. 54

Hambrick, E.P. 51
Hardham, V. 61
Hobson, J. 50
Hughes, D.A. 54
Hunter, M. 60, 61
Huttenlocher, J. 39, 56

Kardiner, A. 45, 139
King, S. 27, 30

Levine, P. 44
Levy, T.M. 37, 52, 55, 58

MacLean, P.D. 41, 42
Minton, K. 36–7, 47–8
Mitchell, J. 58, 67, 134–5
Morgan, R. 25–6

Ogden, P. 36–7, 47–8
Orlans, M. 52, 55, 58

Perry, B.D. 36, 37, 40, 43, 44, 51, 53, 76, 138–9, 140
Philpot, T. 23, 26, 29, 65, 76, 81, 83
Pietromonaco, P.R. 54
Pointon, C. 45

Rees, J. 23
Rose, R. 23, 26, 29, 65, 76, 81, 83
Rowling, J.K. 153, 154
Ryan, T. 23

Schore, A.N. 42, 43, 44, 50, 53, 55, 59
Sgroi, S.M. 129, 130
Shotton, G. 20
Solomon, J. 53
Spiegel, H. 45, 139
Streeck-Fischer, A. 137
Suttie, I.D. 55

Teicher, M.H. 44
Thomas, D.G. 42–3

Van der Kolk, B. 36, 44, 46, 137, 139–40

Walker, R. 23
West, J. 106
Winnicott, D. 53, 60

Ziegler, D. 49

The Child's Own Story
Life Story Work with Traumatized Children

Richard Rose and Terry Philpot
Foreword by Mary Walsh, co-founder and Chief Executive of SACCS
Part of the Delivering Recovery series
Paperback: £15.99 / $29.95
ISBN: 978 1 84310 287 8
160 pages

Helping traumatized children develop the story of their life and the lives of people closest to them is key to their understanding and acceptance of who they are and their past experiences. *The Child's Own Story* is an introduction to life story work and how this effective tool can be used to help children and young people recover from abuse and make sense of a disrupted upbringing in multiple homes or families.

The authors explain the concepts of attachment, separation, loss and identity, using these contexts to describe how to use techniques such as family trees, wallpaper work, and eco- and geno-scaling. They offer guidance on interviewing relatives and carers, and how to gain access to key documentation, including social workers' case files, legal papers, and health, registrar and police records.

This sensitive, practice-focused guide to life story work includes case examples and exercises, and is an invaluable resource for social workers, child psychotherapists, residential care staff, long-term foster carers and other professionals working with traumatized children.

Contents: Foreword, Mary Walsh, Co-founder and Chief Executive of SACCS. 1. Who am I? The Importance of Identity and Meaning. 2. A Tale of Two Children. 3. The Truth and Something Other Than the Truth. 4. Interviewing: Art not Science. 5. Safe at Last: Providing a Safe and Stable Environment. 6. Internalization. 7. Making the Book. 8. But Does it Really Work Like This? 9. Life After Life Story. Appendix: The Story of SACCS. References.

Richard Rose is Deputy Director of Practice Development in SACCS and is responsible for life story work. During his seven years as a senior child protection worker he achieved the Practice Teacher award and a PGCE in social work education. He also has experience in residential care work, and has a PQSW child care award and a BPhil in child care. **Terry Philpot** is author and editor of several books, including (with Anthony Douglas) *Adoption: Changing Families, Changing Times*. He writes regularly for The Times Higher Education Supplement, The Tablet and other publications, and has won several awards for his journalism. He was formerly the editor of Community Care.

Life Story Books for Adopted Children
A Family Friendly Approach

Joy Rees
Foreword by Alan Burnell
Illustrated by Jamie Goldberg
Paperback: £14.99 / $23.95
ISBN: 978 1 84310 953 2
96 pages

Through words, pictures, photographs, certificates and other 'little treasures', a life story book provides a detailed account of the child's early history and a chronology of their life.

This clear and concise book shows a new family-friendly way to compile a life story book that promotes a sense of permanency for the child and encourages attachments within the adoptive family. Joy Rees' improved model works chronologically backwards rather than forwards, aiming to reinforce the child's sense of belonging and security within the adoptive family before addressing the child's past and early trauma. The book contains simple explanations of complex concepts, practical examples and helpful suggestions.

Perfect for busy social workers in local authority children and adoption teams, approved adoption agencies and adoptive parents, *Life Story Books for Adopted Children* is a refreshing, innovative and common-sense guide.

Contents: Foreword. Introduction. 1. A New Approach. 2. A Life Story Book is Not... 3. A Different Perspective. 4. The Inner Child and Subliminal Messages. 5. Involving Adoptive Parents. 6. Compiling the Book. 7. Sample Life Story Book: Danny's Life Adventure. 8. Final Thoughts. References. Further Reading. Index.

Joy Rees is an adoption support worker in a local authority adoption and permanence team in the London borough of Merton, and a Family Futures Associate. She has 30 years' experience as a social worker specialising in children and family work.

Empathic Care for Children with Disorganized Attachments
A Model for Mentalizing, Attachment and Trauma-Informed Care

Chris Taylor
Paperback: £18.99 / $29.95
ISBN: 978 1 84905 182 8
176 pages

Disorganized attachment is the most extreme form of insecure attachment. This book is a practical guide to caring for children and young people with disorganized attachment and related emotional and psychological difficulties.

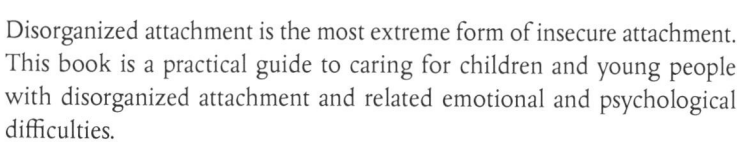

Synthesising attachment, trauma and mentalization theory into a useful practice model, *Empathic Care for Children with Disorganized Attachments* proposes ways of meeting the needs arising in children and young people with disorganized attachments. Focusing on the importance of interpersonal bonds to facilitate the child's capacity to mentalize, it aims to equip the reader with the appropriate skills to provide effective, sustained and, most importantly, empathic care to the most vulnerable and troubled children. This structured psychotherapeutic approach to caregiving will enable the development of child-carer relationships and can be used to create informed, safe environments that support both the young person and the caregiver.

This useful guide will be invaluable to health and social care professionals including residential carers, therapists, counsellors, and those working with vulnerable and troubled children and young people including those supporting foster and adoptive families.

Contents: Acknowledgements. Introduction. 1. A Recovery Model. 2. Attachment. 3. Trauma. 4. A Mentalizing Approach. 5. Attachment and Trauma-Informed Care. 6. Interventions for Attachment Style. 7. Mentalizing and Emotional Arousal. 8. Plan, Do, Reflect, Review. Appendix. Community of Communities: Core Values. References. Index.

Chris Taylor is Clinical Service Manager at Bryn Melyn Care, where he is also a company trainer. He has specialized for over 20 years in working with young people with attachment disorganization and developmental trauma, and delivers training on the subject to foster carers, social workers and residential childcare workers. He teaches Applied Attachment at Glyndwr University, where he is undertaking doctoral research into mentalizing and disorganized attachment. He is also the author of *A Practical Guide to Caring for Children and Teenagers with Attachment Difficulties*, also published by Jessica Kingsley Publishers.